RESEARCH METHODOLOGY

DR ANIL KUMAR GREWAL

CMA AJAY JAIN

This book is dedicated to all the curious minds seeking to unravel the mysteries of research,
To the mentors who guide with wisdom and patience,
To the students who inspire with their relentless pursuit of knowledge,
And to our families, whose unwavering support and encouragement have made this endeavor possible.

Dr. Anil Kumar Grewal
CMA Ajay Jain

Contents

Foreword   *vii*

Preface   *ix*

Acknowledgements   *xi*

Prologue   *xiii*

1. Understanding Research   1

2. Types Of Research   6

3. Defining And Formulating Research Problems   12

4. Conceptual Frameworks And Literature Review   19

5. Formulating Research Objectives And Hypotheses   27

6. Research Design And Methodology   35

7. Sampling Techniques And Data Collection Methods   44

8. Data Analysis And Interpretation   53

9. Reporting And Presenting Research Findings   86

10. Research Ethics   94

11. Advanced Research Techniques And Emerging Methodologies   101

12. The Future Of Research In A Globalized And Technology-Driven World   109

13. Writing A Research Proposal   114

14. Writing And Publishing Research Papers   120

15. Research Dissemination And Impact   126

Epilogue: Embarking on Your Research Journey   133

Foreword

In an era defined by rapid technological advancements and dynamic socio-economic changes, the importance of research as a tool for understanding and solving real-world problems cannot be overstated. Research bridges the gap between knowledge and application, providing a structured approach to uncovering insights and making informed decisions.

It is with this understanding that Research Methodology by Dr. Anil Kumar Grewal and CMA Ajay Jain emerges as a pivotal resource. This book is a comprehensive guide that seamlessly combines theoretical underpinnings with practical applications, catering to the needs of students, educators, and professionals alike. Its well-organized chapters cover the breadth of research, from understanding its foundations to applying it in diverse contexts such as management, social sciences, and beyond.

What sets this work apart is its contextual relevance. Drawing from examples in both Indian and global settings, the authors ensure that the content resonates with a wide audience. Whether you're a student embarking on your first research project or an experienced scholar seeking to refine your methods, this book is an invaluable companion.

I commend the authors for their meticulous effort in crafting a resource that not only educates but also inspires critical thinking and innovation. It is my sincere hope that this book will empower its readers to contribute meaningfully to the body of knowledge in their respective fields.

With best wishes,

Dr. Anil Kumar Grewal

    & CMA Ajay Jain

    Assistant Professor

    Management Education & Research Institute, New Delhi

Preface

In an increasingly interconnected and dynamic world, research has become the cornerstone of informed decision-making, policy formulation, and knowledge expansion. The ability to systematically investigate, analyze, and interpret data is not just a scholarly pursuit—it is an essential skill for solving real-world problems and advancing society. This book, "Research Methodology," is designed to equip students, educators, and practitioners with the foundational and practical knowledge needed to conduct meaningful research across diverse fields.

The book begins by introducing the fundamentals of research, emphasizing its systematic nature and relevance in addressing critical challenges. It then delves into the intricacies of formulating research problems, constructing hypotheses, and designing studies. By balancing theoretical insights with practical applications, the book bridges the gap between academic understanding and real-world implementation.

A key strength of this book lies in its structured approach to explaining research methodologies, including qualitative, quantitative, and mixed-methods approaches. The chapters are enriched with examples, case studies, and scenarios that make complex concepts accessible and relatable. The inclusion of measurement scales, sampling techniques, data analysis methods, and ethical considerations ensures a comprehensive understanding of the research process.

What sets this book apart is its focus on contextual relevance. By incorporating examples and applications drawn from Indian contexts, it addresses the unique challenges and opportunities present in the region. From understanding rural market behaviors to analyzing urban development trends, the book provides insights that are both globally informed and locally pertinent.

I extend my heartfelt gratitude to the mentors, colleagues, and students who have contributed to this work. Their insights and feedback have been instrumental in shaping the content of this book. I also acknowledge my family for their unwavering support and encouragement throughout this journey.

This book is intended to serve as a valuable resource for students, educators, and professionals embarking on their research journeys. It is my sincere hope that it inspires curiosity, critical thinking, and a commitment to excellence in research.

Dr. Anil Kumar Grewal
& CMA Ajay Jain
Assistant Professor
Management Education and Research Institute, New Delhi

Acknowledgements

Writing this book has been a journey of discovery and collaboration, and we are deeply grateful to everyone who has contributed to its creation.

We are profoundly thankful to our families for their unwavering support and understanding throughout this journey. Your patience and belief in our vision have been our greatest source of strength.

We also express our gratitude to Notion Press, Inc., for providing us with the platform and guidance to bring this book to life. Their professionalism and dedication to excellence have been truly inspiring.

To the researchers and scholars whose works we have referenced, we owe our deepest respect and appreciation. Your contributions to the field have paved the way for this endeavor.

Finally, we acknowledge the countless readers, educators, and practitioners who inspire us with their passion for learning and their commitment to applying knowledge to solve real-world problems. It is for you that we write, and it is our hope that this book will serve as a valuable resource on your journey.

With gratitude,

Dr. Anil Kumar Grewal

CMA Ajay Jain

Prologue

In a world driven by data, evidence-based decisions, and continuous innovation, research has emerged as a fundamental pillar of progress. It transcends academic boundaries, influencing policy-making, business strategies, and solutions to societal challenges. Yet, for many, the process of research can seem daunting—an intricate web of methodologies, theories, and analyses.

This book, Research Methodology, was born out of a desire to demystify this process and provide a clear, structured guide for aspiring researchers, educators, and professionals. It is not merely a compilation of concepts but a bridge between theory and application, offering practical insights into how research can be leveraged to understand complex phenomena and drive meaningful change.

Our journey in creating this book has been inspired by countless interactions—with students eager to learn, colleagues sharing their expertise, and the evolving landscape of global challenges demanding innovative solutions. With every chapter, we aim to equip readers with the tools and confidence to embark on their research journey, ensuring that the pursuit of knowledge remains both accessible and rewarding.

The scope of this book spans foundational principles to advanced applications, incorporating diverse examples from India and beyond. By weaving theoretical frameworks with real-world relevance, we hope to provide a resource that resonates with learners and practitioners across disciplines.

As you turn these pages, our hope is that you find not just information but inspiration—a spark to explore, question, and contribute to the ever-expanding realm of human understanding.

Dr. Anil Kumar Grewal

CMA Ajay Jain

CHAPTER I

Understanding Research

Imagine Sneha, a college professor in Mumbai, grappling with a question that haunts her: why are her students disengaged despite her innovative teaching methods? She assumes the problem is students' increasing use of technology. But is this the real cause? Without proper inquiry, her assumptions might mislead her solutions.

One day, she learns about a systematic approach called **research**. She begins by reading literature on student engagement, designing surveys, and conducting interviews. Over time, she realizes that students feel overwhelmed by the fast pace of the syllabus. Armed with this knowledge, Sneha modifies her teaching methods, and student feedback improves significantly.

Sneha's journey illustrates the power of research as a tool to uncover truths, challenge assumptions, and solve real-world problems. This chapter introduces the essence of research—its meaning, importance, characteristics, and how it provides a roadmap for solving pressing issues.

Meaning of Research

Definition

Research is searching again and again. It is the systematic process of investigation designed to expand knowledge, validate already available information, or solve a problem. Research involves the collection, analysis, and interpretation of data by applying scientific or logical methods to derive conclusions or insights. According to Creswell (2014), research involves "steps used to collect and analyze information to increase understanding about a topic or issue."

Meaning

The term "research" derives from the French word *recherche*, meaning "to search again." It highlights the iterative and meticulous nature of uncovering knowledge. Research is far from random data collection—it involves systematic planning, structured execution, and critical analysis to address specific questions or challenges.

For instance, Sneha's effort to explore student disengagement wasn't just casual observation but a structured process involving literature reviews, data collection, and interpretation.

Characteristics of Research

1. Systematic and Structured

Research follows a clear, step-by-step methodology, ensuring each stage is logically connected. For example, a study on customer satisfaction might begin with problem identification, proceed to data collection via surveys, and conclude with an analysis of the results.

2. Objective and Unbiased

Research aims to uncover the truth by minimizing subjective biases. A market researcher studying customer preferences uses structured questions to avoid steering respondents toward a particular answer.

3. Empirical

Empirical research relies on evidence gathered through observation or experimentation, rather than assumptions or intuition. For instance, a sociologist measuring urban migration trends uses census data as an empirical source.

4. Replicable

Good research can be replicated by others under similar conditions, ensuring reliability. If one researcher finds that flexible work hours improve productivity, others must also be able to get the same conclusion if tested.

5. Logical and Analytical

Research uses logical reasoning to analyze data and draw conclusions. For example, studying the correlation between income levels and education requires connecting evidence through logical frameworks.

6. Focused on Problem Solving

Research addresses specific problems or unanswered questions. Whether it's understanding societal issues like poverty or improving organizational practices, research is always solution-oriented.

Why is Research Important in Social Sciences and Management?

Research in social sciences and management plays a critical role in understanding human behavior, designing policies, and making informed decisions.

1. Understanding Complex Human Behavior

In social sciences, research helps decode multifaceted human behavior. For example, psychologists studying workplace stress use research to identify its causes and suggest interventions.

2. Informed Decision-Making

Managers use research to make data-driven decisions. For example, market research conducted by a company to gauge consumer preferences and minimize risks for launching a new product.

3. Policy Formulation

Governments rely on research to craft effective policies. For instance, a study on literacy rates helps identify gaps in education, guiding targeted programs.

4. Problem Solving

Research offers actionable solutions to real-world challenges. For instance, Sneha's problem of disengaged students was resolved through a structured investigation of their needs.

5. Advancing Knowledge

Research contributes to academia by expanding understanding of critical issues, such as income inequality or environmental sustainability. These insights influence both academic discourse and practical applications.

Managerial Value of Research

In today's fast-paced and competitive business landscape, managers rely heavily on research to make informed decisions, address challenges, and seize opportunities. Research acts as a systematic tool for gathering insights that guide strategies in marketing, operations, finance, and human resources. By providing data-backed evidence, research helps reduce uncertainties, ensuring that managerial decisions are not based solely on intuition but on factual analysis.

The Role of Research in Managerial Functions

1. **Strategic Planning:**
   Research supports long-term planning by analyzing market trends, competitor behavior, and customer preferences. For example, Tata Consultancy Services (TCS) conducts research on emerging technologies like blockchain and artificial intelligence to design innovative solutions for their global clients.
2. **Problem Identification and Resolution:**
   Identifying the root causes of business problems is a key managerial responsibility. Research uncovers hidden issues by systematically studying internal and external environments. For instance, Maruti Suzuki used customer feedback surveys to pinpoint dissatisfaction with specific service centers, enabling them to improve customer support.

3. **Market Understanding:**
Comprehensive market research helps managers understand consumer behavior, product preferences, and pricing dynamics. A notable example is Hindustan Unilever's rural market research, which revealed unique buying patterns in small towns, leading to the launch of affordable product variants like sachet shampoos.

4. **Performance Measurement and Improvement:**
Research provides metrics to evaluate the performance of employees, processes, and overall organizational goals. ITC, for instance, uses employee engagement surveys to track workforce satisfaction and refine HR policies accordingly.

5. **Risk Mitigation:**
By analyzing market data and forecasting potential threats, research minimizes risks associated with business expansions, product launches, or investments. Flipkart, before launching its grocery delivery service, conducted a pilot study in select cities to mitigate logistical challenges.

6. **Innovation and Growth:**
Research drives innovation by identifying new opportunities and untapped markets. For example, Zomato invested in customer research to enhance their app's user interface, leading to higher engagement and order volumes.

Case Studies of Managerial Research in India

1. **Amul's Product Diversification:**
Amul leveraged extensive consumer research to identify gaps in the ice cream and flavored milk markets, leading to the launch of Amul Kool and Amul Sugar-Free ice creams. These research-driven innovations catered to changing dietary preferences and expanded Amul's market share.

2. **Reliance Jio's Disruption Strategy:**
Before entering the telecommunications market, Reliance Jio studied consumer dissatisfaction with high data prices and low internet speeds. Their research-driven strategy enabled them to launch affordable data plans, transforming the industry.

Managerial research goes beyond just collecting data—it's about transforming information into actionable strategies. Whether it's reducing costs, launching a new product, or improving customer satisfaction, businesses that prioritize research are better equipped to thrive in competitive markets. In essence, research is the backbone of effective decision-making and a key driver of organizational success.

The Research Process

A structured research process ensures efficiency and reliability. Let's break it down:

1. Problem Identification
First, we need to define the issue (Problem Identification) clearly. For example, an NGO working on health issues might ask, "Why is the vaccination rate low in rural areas?"

2. Reviewing Literature
Next, existing research is studied to identify gaps. For example, studies on vaccination hesitancy might reveal factors like misinformation or logistical challenges.

3. Formulating Hypotheses
Researchers then propose testable hypotheses. For instance:

- Null Hypothesis (H^0): Awareness campaigns do not affect vaccination rates.
- Alternative Hypothesis (H_1): Awareness campaigns increase vaccination rates.

4. Designing the Study

The researcher selects methods like surveys, experiments, or focus groups to collect data. For example, a study might use door-to-door surveys to gather data from rural households.

5. Data Collection

This involves gathering information systematically. Surveys, interviews, and observations are common methods. For instance, collecting data from farmers about their perceptions of government schemes.

6. Data Analysis

Data is analyzed using statistical tools or thematic coding, depending on the type of research. A researcher might use software like SPSS to analyze correlations or Excel for trend analysis.

7. Reporting and Interpretation

Finally, findings are interpreted and presented in reports or publications. Recommendations for policymakers, organizations, or academics are drawn from the results.

Example

A public health researcher studying the spread of dengue might:

- Identify hotspots.
- Analyze factors contributing to mosquito breeding.
- Recommend targeted awareness campaigns and sanitation drives.

Challenges in Research

1. Time and Resource Constraints

Conducting large-scale studies can be time-consuming and expensive. For example, a national survey on education requires significant funding and manpower.

2. Data Collection Issues

Researchers often face low response rates in surveys or incomplete datasets. For instance, rural respondents might be hesitant to share information due to mistrust.

3. Bias in Research

Personal biases can influence interpretations. For example, a researcher with preconceived notions about urban crime might unintentionally skew the study.

4. Ethical Considerations

Research involving human participants must ensure confidentiality and informed consent. For example, studies on mental health must protect sensitive data.

5. Complexity of Human Behavior

Social phenomena are influenced by multiple factors, making them difficult to study conclusively. For instance, studying poverty requires examining economic, cultural, and social dimensions.

Real-World Example

Let's consider the example of a public policy researcher studying rural unemployment:

1. **Problem**: Why is unemployment high in rural areas despite government schemes?
2. **Literature Review**: Analyze existing studies on rural employment trends and scheme implementation.
3. **Hypothesis**: Government training programs improve employment rates.
4. **Design**: Conduct surveys among beneficiaries and non-beneficiaries.
5. **Data Collection**: Use structured interviews to gather opinions on the effectiveness of schemes.
6. **Analysis**: Compare employment rates using statistical tools like chi-square tests.

7. **Reporting**: Publish findings to recommend improvements in skill development initiatives.

Research is more than a tool for gathering information—it's a systematic process for solving problems, advancing knowledge, and driving progress. By following a structured research process, individuals like Sneha or public policy researchers can uncover actionable insights that lead to meaningful change.

The next chapter will explore **types of research**, guiding you on how to choose the most appropriate method for your study.

References

Creswell, J. W. (2014). *Research design: Qualitative, quantitative, and mixed methods approaches* (4th ed.). Sage Publications.

Neuman, W. L. (2014). *Social research methods: Qualitative and quantitative approaches* (7th ed.). Pearson Education.

Bryman, A. (2015). *Social research methods* (5th ed.). Oxford University Press.

Denzin, N. K., & Lincoln, Y. S. (2011). *The SAGE handbook of qualitative research* (4th ed.). Sage Publications.

Kothari, C. R. (2004). *Research methodology: Methods and techniques.* New Age International.

CHAPTER II

Types of Research

Meet Ravi, a Ph.D. student in management who is exploring employee satisfaction in remote workplaces. Initially, Ravi felt lost because the topic seemed vast, and he didn't know how to approach it. His guide advised him to start by deciding the **type of research** he would conduct. Should he explore the reasons behind dissatisfaction using **exploratory research**, measure satisfaction levels with **descriptive research**, or analyze how remote work policies affect satisfaction using **causal research**?

After understanding the types of research, Ravi decided to use **exploratory research** to identify key factors influencing satisfaction. He then moved to **descriptive research** to measure satisfaction levels, followed by **causal research** to test whether flexibility in working hours improves satisfaction. This structured approach helped Ravi conduct meaningful research, yielding actionable insights.

This chapter explains the various types of research, their characteristics, and their applications, guiding you to choose the right type for your research journey.

Introduction to Types of Research

Classification of research into multiple types based on purpose, approach, and time limit can be done. Knowledge of these distinctions helps researchers design studies that are effective, reliable, and aligned with their objectives. Each type has its own strengths, limitations, and areas of application, as explained below.

1. Research Based on Purpose

This classification is focused on **why** the research is conducted and **what** it aims to achieve.

Exploratory Research

Definition: Exploratory research is conducted when there is little existing knowledge about a topic. It is used to identify new ideas, generate hypotheses, or explore phenomena without predefined outcomes.

Example in Social Sciences: Imagine a sociologist studying how gig economy workers perceive job security. Since this is an emerging area with limited prior research, exploratory methods such as open-ended interviews and focus groups can uncover workers' attitudes, challenges, and expectations.

Methods Used:

1. **Literature Reviews**: Reviewing existing but limited information to identify gaps.
2. **Focus Groups**: Discussing topics with small groups to generate insights.
3. **Interviews**: Conducting unstructured interviews to explore subjective perspectives.

Key Characteristics:

1. Flexible and adaptive in design.
2. Relies on qualitative data.
3. Provides the foundation for future research.

Real-World Example: Tech startups exploring user needs for AI-based educational tools use exploratory research to identify key features that users might value, such as personalized learning recommendations.

Descriptive Research

Definition: Descriptive research aims to systematically describe a phenomenon, group, or situation without investigating cause-and-effect relationships.

Example in Management: A study profiling Indian millennials who use online food delivery apps. The research could describe demographic factors like age, income, preferences, and spending patterns.

Methods Used:

1. **Surveys**: Questionnaires to collect structured data from large groups.
2. **Observations**: Monitoring specific behaviors in real-world settings.
3. **Case Studies**: Detailed examinations of a single entity or phenomenon.

Key Characteristics:

1. Answers the "who," "what," "when," and "where" questions but not "why."
2. Uses structured methods to collect reliable data.
3. Often serves as a precursor to causal research.

Real-World Example: Descriptive research on customer complaints at a bank might categorize issues (e.g., service delays, app glitches) and quantify their frequency. This provides actionable insights into areas requiring immediate attention.

Causal Research

Definition: Causal research examines cause-and-effect relationships by testing specific hypotheses. It is highly structured and often involves experiments or advanced statistical methods.

Example in Management: A company tests whether offering free gym memberships to employees improves their productivity. The research compares productivity levels before and after implementing the policy.

Methods Used:

1. **Controlled Experiments**: Manipulating one variable while keeping others constant.
2. **Regression Analysis**: Measuring the effect of one variable on another statistically.

Key Characteristics:

1. Focuses on determining causality, not just correlation.
2. Requires careful control of external factors.
3. Produces actionable results for decision-making.

Real-World Example: An e-commerce platform studies whether changing the color of its "Buy Now" button from brown to green has any impact on the volume of sales. By running A/B tests (showing users different versions), it measures the causal impact of button color on purchase behavior.

Proposition and Hypothesis in Research

Propositions and hypotheses are critical elements of research design. While they are closely related, they serve distinct purposes in guiding research studies. Understanding these concepts is essential for designing effective studies and testing relationships between variables.

What is a Proposition?

A proposition is a declarative statement that predicts a general relationship between concepts or variables. It serves as a foundational assumption or starting point for further investigation. Unlike a hypothesis, a proposition is broader and not necessarily testable directly.

Example of a Proposition:
"Increasing employee engagement leads to improved organizational performance."
In the context of Indian businesses:
Case Study: A proposition could be applied in a study examining how Reliance Industries' investment in employee training programs has improved productivity across its various verticals.
Characteristics of a Proposition:

1. **Broad in Scope:** Propositions establish general relationships without focusing on specific variables.
2. **Theoretical Basis:** Derived from existing theories, they act as a guiding framework for further research.
3. **Not Immediately Testable:** Propositions may require refinement or narrowing to develop testable hypotheses.

What is a Hypothesis?
A hypothesis, on the other hand, is a specific, testable statement that predicts the relationship between two or more variables. It refines propositions into measurable components and forms the basis for empirical testing.
Types of Hypotheses:

1. **Null Hypothesis (H^0):** Assumes no relationship or effect between variables.

   ◦ Example: "There is no significant relationship between employee satisfaction and retention rates in IT companies in Bengaluru."

2. **Alternative Hypothesis (H_1):** Suggests there is a relationship or effect.

   ◦ Example: "Higher employee satisfaction significantly improves retention rates in IT companies in Bengaluru."

Characteristics of a Hypothesis:

1. **Testable:** A hypothesis must be measurable through observation or experimentation.
2. **Specific:** Focuses on well-defined variables and their interactions.
3. **Predictive:** Offers a clear prediction about outcomes.

Steps to Develop Hypotheses

1. **Review Literature:** Study existing research to identify gaps or areas needing exploration.

   ◦ Example: Analyze studies on employee turnover to hypothesize why startups in India face higher attrition rates.

2. **Define Variables:** Clearly distinguish independent (cause) and dependent (effect) variables.

   ◦ Independent Variable: Flexible work policies.
   ◦ Dependent Variable: Employee productivity.

3. **Formulate Null and Alternative Hypotheses:** Ensure they are clear and aligned with the research objectives.

   Example:

- **Null Hypothesis (H^0):** Flexible work policies do not significantly affect employee productivity.

- **Alternative Hypothesis** (H_1): Flexible work policies significantly improve employee productivity.

Real-World Application: Propositions and Hypotheses in Indian Industry

1. **Proposition Example:** "Increased adoption of AI in Indian businesses enhances operational efficiency."

   - Application: Infosys might test this proposition by studying how its AI tools streamline project timelines.

2. **Hypothesis Example:** "AI adoption reduces project completion time by 20% in Indian IT firms."

   - Testing Method: Data collection and analysis of project timelines before and after AI implementation.

Importance of Propositions and Hypotheses

1. **Guiding Research:** Propositions frame the broader inquiry, while hypotheses focus on specific testable aspects.
2. **Validating Theories:** Hypotheses provide a mechanism to confirm or refute theoretical assumptions.
3. **Driving Innovation:** In industries like e-commerce, propositions about customer behavior are tested using hypotheses to develop personalized recommendations.

2. Research Based on Approach

Research can also be classified based on the methods used to collect and analyze data. The three main approaches are **qualitative**, **quantitative**, and **mixed methods**.

Qualitative Research

Definition: Qualitative research focuses on understanding human experiences, perceptions, and emotions through non-numeric data.

Example in Social Sciences: A study analyzing the narratives of domestic workers in urban India to understand their challenges and aspirations.

Methods Used:

1. **In-depth Interviews:** Gathering rich, detailed information from participants.
2. **Ethnography:** Immersing in participants' daily lives to observe behaviors.
3. **Content Analysis:** Analyzing text, images, or videos for recurring themes.

Key Characteristics:

1. Relies on open-ended questions and unstructured methods.
2. Produces detailed, context-rich data.
3. Subjective in interpretation but offers deep insights.

Real-World Example: Qualitative research might explore how rural women perceive microfinance programs, identifying barriers like lack of trust in financial institutions.

Quantitative Research

Definition: Quantitative research uses numerical data to measure phenomena and test hypotheses. It is structured, objective, and often involves statistical analysis.

Example in Management: A survey of 1,000 customers measuring satisfaction with a company's services using a 5-point Likert scale.

Methods Used:

1. **Surveys**: Structured questionnaires with close-ended questions.
2. **Experiments**: Controlled studies testing specific variables.
3. **Secondary Data Analysis**: Analyzing existing data sources like government reports.

Key Characteristics:

1. Results are generalizable to larger populations.
2. Emphasizes objectivity and replicability.
3. Uses tools like SPSS, R, or Excel for data analysis.

Real-World Example: Quantitative research on employee engagement might measure engagement levels across departments and correlate them with performance metrics.

Mixed-Methods Research

Definition: Mixed-methods research utilizes both qualitative and quantitative approaches to provide a comprehensive understanding of a topic.

Example in Social Sciences: A study on the impact of remote work might include surveys (quantitative) to measure productivity and interviews (qualitative) to explore employee experiences.

Methods Used:

1. Combining structured surveys with open-ended interviews.
2. Triangulating data to validate findings.

Key Characteristics:

1. Integrates the strengths of both approaches.
2. Produces more nuanced insights.
3. Demands expertise in multiple methodologies.

Real-World Example: A mixed-methods study on e-learning could analyze survey results for trends in student satisfaction while using interviews to understand challenges faced during online classes.

3. Research Based on Timeframe

Research can also be categorized based on its duration and the frequency of data collection.

One-Time Survey Research

Definition: One-Time Survey Research is a type of observational study that analyzes data collected from a population or a representative subset at a specific point in time. It aims to identify the prevalence of certain characteristics, behaviors, or conditions and explore associations between variables without determining causal relationships. This approach provides a "snapshot" of the population, making it ideal for studying trends, differences among groups, or the distribution of phenomena within a given timeframe.

Example in Management: A one-time survey measuring customer satisfaction with online banking services conducted in March 2023.

Key Characteristics:

1. Cost-effective and time-efficient.
2. Provides a snapshot of a specific moment.

3. Limited in explaining changes or trends over time.

Real-World Example: Cross-sectional research might analyze the prevalence of hybrid work models in Indian companies during the COVID-19 pandemic.

Longitudinal Research

Definition: Longitudinal research tracks changes over time by collecting data at multiple intervals.

Example in Social Sciences: Tracking the progress of rural women entrepreneurs in India over five years to measure the impact of government schemes.

Key Characteristics:

1. Provides insights into trends and changes.
2. Requires significant time and financial investment.
3. More robust for studying cause-and-effect relationships.

Real-World Example: A longitudinal study might analyze changes in consumer spending patterns across economic cycles (e.g., pre-pandemic, during the pandemic, and post-pandemic).

The type of research you choose determines how effectively you address your research objectives. Whether it's **exploratory**, **descriptive**, or **causal**; **qualitative** or **quantitative**; **cross-sectional** or **longitudinal**, each type has unique strengths and applications. As Ravi discovered, understanding these distinctions helps you structure your study systematically, leading to meaningful and actionable outcomes.

In the next chapter, we will delve deeper into the process of identifying and defining research problems, the starting point of any impactful research journey.

References

Bryman, A. (2015). *Social research methods* (5th ed.). Oxford University Press.

Creswell, J. W. (2014). *Research design: Qualitative, quantitative, and mixed methods approaches* (4th ed.). Sage Publications.

Neuman, W. L. (2014). *Social research methods: Qualitative and quantitative approaches* (7th ed.). Pearson Education.

Tashakkori, A., & Teddlie, C. (2010). *SAGE handbook of mixed methods in social & behavioral research*. Sage Publications.

CHAPTER III

Defining and Formulating Research Problems

Rohan, a management researcher, wanted to study why employees leave startups within their first year. He assumed the reasons were low salaries and long working hours. Excited, he started collecting data and conducting interviews. However, when presenting his preliminary findings, his mentor pointed out a glaring issue: Rohan had not clearly defined the research problem. He realized he was focusing on his assumptions rather than framing an unbiased, well-structured problem statement.

After revisiting his approach, Rohan identified his core research problem as: **"What factors contribute to high employee turnover in startups within the first year of employment?"** This clarity helped him design surveys, gather relevant data, and generate insights that were actionable for startup HR managers.

Rohan's story illustrates that the success of any research hinges on a well-defined problem. This chapter focuses on the meaning, characteristics, and steps to identify and formulate research problems in social sciences and management.

What is a Research Problem?

Definition

Research Problem: A perplexing situation, condition, or issue that exists in scholarly literature, in theory, or in practice that points to the need for meaningful understanding and deliberate investigation. Kothari (2004)opined that a research problem is "a question that requires an answer to resolve ambiguity, inconsistency, or an incomplete understanding of a phenomenon."

Importance of Defining a Research Problem

A poorly defined problem leads to unclear objectives, flawed methodologies, and irrelevant conclusions. A well-defined research problem acts as a compass, ensuring that all aspects of the study—data collection, analysis, and reporting—are aligned.

Characteristics of a Good Research Problem

1. **Specific and Focused**

   - A good research problem should be narrow enough to explore within the available time and resources.
   - For instance, instead of studying "Employee Satisfaction," a more focused problem might be: **"What role does managerial feedback play in enhancing employee satisfaction in IT startups?"**

2. **Relevant and Significant**

   - The problem should address an important issue that contributes to knowledge or solves a practical challenge.
   - Example: A study exploring rural women's access to microfinance can have significant implications for policy design and poverty reduction.

3. **Researchable**

   - The problem must be feasible to investigate using available tools and methods.
   - Example: A study on the effects of work-from-home policies during the COVID-19 pandemic is researchable using surveys and employee productivity data.

4. **Based on Gaps in Knowledge**

   - A good research problem arises from gaps identified in existing literature.
   - Example: If previous studies on customer loyalty only focus on urban areas, a researcher could explore loyalty behaviors in rural markets.

5. **Ethically Sound**

   - The problem should respect participants' rights and avoid causing harm.
   - Example: A study on workplace harassment must ensure confidentiality and informed consent from participants.

Sources of Research Problems

1. Personal Experience

Researchers often derive problems from their observations or challenges faced in daily life.

- **Example**: A manager experiencing high employee absenteeism may investigate its underlying causes.

2. Existing Literature

Reviewing prior studies helps identify gaps or unresolved issues.

- **Example**: A literature review on remote work might reveal that little research has been done on its impact on team collaboration.

3. Practical Problems in Society

Real-world challenges often serve as a rich source of research problems.

- **Example**: Studying why government welfare schemes fail to reach marginalized communities.

4. Discussions with Experts

Conversations with mentors, industry professionals, or peers can spark ideas for research problems.

- **Example**: An HR consultant might suggest studying the link between flexible benefits and employee retention.

5. Policy Gaps

Unresolved issues in policies or programs offer opportunities for research.

- **Example**: Examining why environmental protection laws are poorly enforced in urban areas.

  Steps to Identify a Research Problem
  Step 1: Identify a Broad Area of Interest

- Begin by exploring topics that align with your field and interests.
- Example: A researcher interested in education might start with "teacher performance."

  Step 2: Conduct a Literature Review

- Study existing research to understand what has already been explored and where gaps lie.
- Example: Literature might reveal that while teacher motivation has been studied, the role of school leadership in enhancing teacher performance remains unexplored.

  Step 3: Narrow Down the Scope

- Focus on a specific aspect of the topic to make it manageable.
- Example: Instead of studying "teacher performance," focus on **"the impact of school leadership on teacher motivation in government schools."**

  Step 4: Assess Viability

- Consider availability of time, resources, and skills required to solve the problem.
- Example: A researcher planning a nationwide survey must ensure sufficient funding and manpower.

  Step 5: Define the Problem Statement

- Frame the problem as a clear and concise statement or question.
- Example: **"How does school leadership influence teacher motivation in government schools of rural India?"**

Importance of Problem Definition in Research

Defining a research problem is the foundation of any successful study. Without a well-articulated problem, the entire research process risks being misaligned, leading to irrelevant or invalid results. A clearly defined problem ensures that the research objectives, methodology, and analysis stay focused and actionable.

Key Reasons Why Problem Definition is Crucial

1. **Aligns Research Objectives with Purpose**
   A well-defined problem statement bridges the gap between the research question and its objectives. For example, a startup struggling with high customer churn might initially identify "poor marketing" as the issue. However,

through detailed research, the actual problem might be found to be inadequate customer support.

- ◦ **Example in India:** Flipkart analyzed its customer retention challenges and discovered that delivery delays were a bigger issue than product variety. This insight led to investment in last-mile logistics.

2. **Focuses Efforts and Resources**
   Proper problem definition helps prioritize tasks and allocate resources effectively. For instance, research on improving agricultural productivity in India should focus on specific bottlenecks, such as irrigation or fertilizer access, rather than a broad scope of "low productivity."
3. **Enables Better Methodological Design**
   An ill-defined problem often leads to mismatched research methods. For example, studying employee morale without specifying the factors (e.g., salaries, work culture) would result in vague conclusions. A clear problem definition ensures that tools like surveys or experiments are tailored to research needs.
4. **Avoids Bias and Assumptions**
   Defining the problem ensures the researcher doesn't start with unfounded assumptions. For example, assuming "low pay" is the main reason for employee attrition might overlook factors like lack of recognition or poor management.

   - ◦ **Case Example:** Infosys conducted in-depth research on its employee attrition rate, which revealed that skill development opportunities were a bigger concern than salary.

5. **Enhances Decision-Making Relevance**
   Research rooted in a clear problem statement provides actionable insights for decision-makers. In industries like retail or telecom, this clarity can directly influence market strategies.
6. **Facilitates Collaboration and Communication**
   When multiple stakeholders are involved in a study, a clearly defined problem ensures everyone understands the research's purpose. For instance, a government project on reducing urban traffic congestion must clearly articulate whether the focus is on public transport usage or traffic management systems.

Common Challenges in Defining Research Problems

1. **Vagueness in Scope:**
   A problem like "Why are people dissatisfied with urban living?" is too broad. Instead, narrowing it down to "What factors contribute to dissatisfaction with public transport in Delhi?" makes it actionable.
2. **Overlooking Contextual Factors:**
   Problems must be contextualized to the environment in which the study is conducted. For example, studying rural unemployment in Bihar requires consideration of unique socio-economic factors like migration patterns and seasonal employment.
3. **Complexity in Multi-Factor Scenarios:**
   When problems involve multiple variables, it's essential to prioritize key drivers. For instance, studying low agricultural yields might focus first on irrigation, and later expand to soil fertility and crop rotation practices.

Real-World Examples from India

1. **Policy Formulation:**
   The government's Swachh Bharat Mission succeeded partly because its problem statement— "lack of sanitation in rural India"—was clearly defined. This focus enabled targeted interventions like constructing toilets and spreading awareness.

2. **Corporate Strategy:**
   Zomato faced declining customer engagement in specific cities. Research revealed the root cause was inconsistent delivery times, not competition or pricing. By addressing this specific problem, Zomato improved its operational efficiency.

3. **Educational Reform:**
   Research on poor student performance in government schools in Uttar Pradesh identified "lack of teacher attendance" as the primary issue rather than infrastructure deficiencies. This clarity drove effective interventions.

   The process of defining a research problem

ensures that the study remains focused, relevant, and impactful. Whether it is addressing operational challenges, formulating policies, or improving societal outcomes, a well-defined problem acts as the cornerstone for deriving meaningful insights and actionable recommendations. In essence, problem definition is not just the starting point but the compass that directs every stage of the research process.

Formulating a Problem Statement

A problem statement articulates the research problem in a clear and concise way. It serves as the foundation for developing research objectives and hypotheses.

Structure of a Problem Statement

1. **Context**: Provide background information to introduce the problem.

   - Example: "Employee turnover rates in Indian startups are significantly higher than in established companies."

2. **Gap**: Highlight what is unknown or unresolved.

   - Example: "While previous studies focus on financial incentives, little is known about the impact of work culture on employee retention."

3. **Purpose**: State the aim of investigation of the study.

   - Example: "This study aims to investigate the role of organizational culture in reducing employee turnover in startups."

Example of a Research Problem

Context

The agricultural sector in India employs more than 50% of the population but contributes less than 20% to GDP. Small farmers face challenges like low productivity, lack of market access, and inefficient supply chains.

Gap

While previous studies focus on government schemes, few explore the role of private interventions in solving these challenges.

Purpose

This study aims to examine the effectiveness of private-sector initiatives in improving market access for small farmers in Maharashtra.

Problem Statement: "What role do private-sector interventions play in enhancing market access for small-scale farmers in Maharashtra?"

Common Mistakes in Defining Research Problems

1. **Vague or Overly Broad Problems**

   - Example: "Why are people unhappy with public transport?"
   - Solution: Narrow it down to specifics, such as "What factors influence commuter satisfaction with public buses in Mumbai?"

2. **Focusing on Assumptions Rather Than Facts**

   - Example: Assuming that low salaries are the primary reason for employee turnover without evidence.
   - Solution: Use exploratory research to identify actual factors first.

3. **Irrelevant or Insignificant Problems**

   - Example: Studying the popularity of a niche product with limited applicability.
   - Solution: Ensure the problem has practical significance or contributes to knowledge.

4. **Unethical Problems**

   - Example: Researching sensitive topics like mental health without ensuring confidentiality.
   - Solution: Follow ethical guidelines to protect participants.

Real-World Applications of Research Problems

1. **Social Sciences**: Understanding the root causes of gender disparity in higher education enrollment.
2. **Management**: Exploring the effectiveness of performance appraisal systems in IT companies.
3. **Economics**: Investigating the impact of inflation on household savings in rural areas.
4. **Public Health**: Studying barriers to vaccination in underserved communities.

Defining and formulating a research problem is the cornerstone of any successful study. Without a clear, specific, and researchable problem, the entire research process can lose direction. As seen in Rohan's case, investing time in framing the problem ensures clarity and focus, guiding every subsequent step. In the next chapter, we will explore conceptual frameworks and literature reviews—essential tools for understanding and contextualizing your research problem.

References

Bryman, A. (2015). *Social research methods* (5th ed.). Oxford University Press.
Creswell, J. W. (2014). *Research design: Qualitative, quantitative, and mixed methods approaches* (4th ed.). Sage Publications.
Kothari, C. R. (2004). *Research methodology: Methods and techniques.* New Age International.
Neuman, W. L. (2014). *Social research methods: Qualitative and quantitative approaches* (7th ed.). Pearson Education.
Robson, C. (2007). *How to do a research project: A guide for undergraduate students.* Blackwell Publishing.

CHAPTER IV

Conceptual Frameworks and Literature Review

Amrita, a postgraduate student in social sciences, was examining the Relationship Between Leadership Styles and Employee Outcomes in Small Businesses She eagerly started collecting data, designing surveys, and interviewing employees. However, her supervisor stopped her midway and asked, "How are you framing your study? What's your conceptual framework?" Amrita was puzzled.

Her supervisor explained that without understanding existing theories and creating a conceptual framework, her research would lack depth and context. She needed to review the literature, define variables, and structure her ideas around a framework. This helped her connect her research to existing studies and clarify the relationships between leadership styles, motivation, and performance.

Amrita's story underscores the importance of conceptual frameworks and literature reviews in anchoring research to established knowledge. This chapter explores these two essential components in depth.

What is a Conceptual Framework?

A **conceptual framework** is a visual or written representation of the relationships between variables in a study. It explains how the researcher expects these variables to interact, based on prior knowledge and existing theories.

Definition

In the opinion of Miles and Huberman (1994), a conceptual framework is "a visual or written product that explains, either graphically or in narrative form, the main things to be studied, the key factors, concepts, or variables, and the presumed relationships among them."

Purpose of a Conceptual Framework

1. **Clarifies Relationships Between Variables**

   - It specifies how independent variables (e.g., leadership styles) affect dependent variables (e.g., employee performance).
   - Example: A researcher studying stress might link workplace conditions (independent variable) to employee burnout (dependent variable).

2. **Guides Data Collection and Analysis**

   - The framework determines which data to collect and which analysis methods to use.
   - Example: If your framework emphasizes motivation as a mediator, you'll design surveys to measure both leadership styles and motivation.

3. **Connects the Study to Theoretical Foundations**

   - It helps ground your research in established theories, making your findings more credible.
   - Example: Using Herzberg's Two-Factor Theory to study job satisfaction links your research to existing models.

4. **Helps in Hypothesis Development**

- A conceptual framework allows researchers to derive testable hypotheses.
- Example: **Hypothesis**: Transformational leadership improves employee creativity through increased motivation.

5. Simplifies Complex Relationships

- By visually organizing variables, frameworks simplify how complex interactions are presented.

Components of a Conceptual Framework

1. **Independent Variables**: Factors that influence or cause changes (e.g., leadership style).
2. **Dependent Variables**: Outcomes that the research seeks to explain (e.g., employee performance).
3. **Mediators and Moderators**: Variables that affect the strength or direction of the relationship between cause and effect.

    ◦ Example: Motivation might mediate the effect of leadership on performance.

4. **Theoretical Basis**: Theories or models that support your framework.

Example of a Conceptual Framework

Study Topic: The Effect of Leadership Style on Employee Performance
    Variables:

- Independent Variable: Leadership Style (transformational, transactional)
- Dependent Variable: Employee Performance
- Mediating Variable: Motivation

Visual Framework:
Leadership Style → Motivation → Employee Performance
Measurement Scales in Research
Measurement scales are fundamental to designing surveys and analyzing data. They determine how variables are categorized, recorded, and interpreted in a study. Choosing the right scale ensures accurate data collection and analysis, enabling researchers to derive meaningful conclusions.
Types of Measurement Scales
There are four major types of measurement scales used in research: **Nominal, Ordinal, Interval, and Ratio.** Each scale has unique characteristics and applications.
1. Nominal Scale
The nominal scale is the simplest level of measurement. It categorizes data into distinct groups that do not have a specific order.

- **Characteristics**:

    ◦ Categories are mutually exclusive (no overlap).

- No inherent ranking or numerical value.
- Can only be analyzed using frequency counts or percentages.

- **Examples in Research:**

  - Gender (Male, Female, Other)
  - Regions (North, South, East, West)

- **Application in India:**

  - A survey studying voter preferences could use a nominal scale to classify respondents by state (e.g., Uttar Pradesh, Maharashtra, Gujarat).

2. Ordinal Scale
The ordinal scale categorizes data into ranked order, but the intervals between ranks are not equal or defined.

- **Characteristics:**

  - Data is ranked or ordered.
  - Differences between ranks are not measurable or uniform.
  - Useful for subjective assessments.

- **Examples in Research:**

  - Customer satisfaction ratings (Very Dissatisfied, Dissatisfied, Neutral, Satisfied, Very Satisfied)
  - Educational qualification (High School, Undergraduate, Postgraduate)

- **Application in India:**

  - An e-commerce company like Flipkart might use an ordinal scale to rate delivery satisfaction (1 to 5 stars).

3. Interval Scale
The interval scale provides a ranked order with equal intervals between data points, but it lacks a true zero point.

- **Characteristics:**

  - Differences between values are meaningful and measurable.
  - Cannot calculate true ratios (e.g., twice as much).
  - Negative values are possible.

- **Examples in Research:**

  - Temperature measured in Celsius or Fahrenheit.
  - Likert-scale questions in surveys (e.g., "On a scale of 1 to 7, how satisfied are you?").

- **Application in India:**

- A market research study on smartphone preferences might use an interval scale to measure respondents' likelihood to recommend a brand (e.g., 1 = Very Unlikely, 7 = Very Likely).

4. Ratio Scale

The ratio scale is the highest level of measurement. It has an absolute zero point and equal intervals, allowing for meaningful comparisons and calculations of ratios.

- **Characteristics:**

  - Includes all properties of nominal, ordinal, and interval scales.
  - True zero point exists (absence of the property being measured).
  - Allows for operations like multiplication and division.

- **Examples in Research:**

  - Income levels (in rupees)
  - Age (in years)
  - Weight (in kilograms)

- **Application in India:**

  - A study measuring agricultural productivity in Maharashtra might use a ratio scale for variables like crop yield per hectare.

Choosing the Right Scale

The choice of measurement scale depends on the research objectives, the type of data being collected, and the statistical analysis required. For instance:

- **Nominal and ordinal scales** are ideal for qualitative or categorical data.
- **Interval and ratio scales** are suited for quantitative data requiring precise measurements.

Importance of Measurement Scales in Research

1. **Accuracy and Precision:** The appropriate scale ensures that data is captured in a form suitable for analysis.
2. **Applicability to Statistical Tools:** Advanced statistical tests (e.g., regression, ANOVA) often require interval or ratio scales.
3. **Clarity in Surveys:** Proper scales improve the design of survey instruments, reducing respondent confusion.
4. **Data Comparability:** Consistent use of scales allows for better comparison across studies.

Real-World Applications in Indian Research

1. **Healthcare Studies:** A hospital in Delhi might use an ordinal scale to measure patient satisfaction levels and a ratio scale to track treatment success rates (e.g., survival rates).
2. **Education Research:** A study in Rajasthan could use an interval scale to assess students' perceptions of online education and a nominal scale to classify schools by region.

The Literature Review

A literature review systematically analyzes and synthesizes existing research relevant to your research area. It identifies gaps, connects your research to prior work, and establishes a foundation for your study.

Importance of a Literature Review

1. **Provides Context and Background**

   - The literature review sets the stage by explaining what is already known about the topic.
   - Example: Reviewing studies on employee performance might reveal that leadership style is a recurring factor, justifying its inclusion in your research.

2. **Identifies Research Gaps**

   - It highlights unanswered questions or areas needing further investigation.
   - Example: If previous studies on leadership styles focus on large organizations, a gap exists for small businesses.

3. **Justifies Your Research**

   - A well-done review shows how your study contributes to the field.
   - Example: Your research might explore how remote leadership influences performance, a topic not yet extensively studied.

4. **Informs Methodology**

   - By studying existing methods, you can adopt or refine techniques used in prior research.
   - Example: If earlier studies used structured interviews, you might use the same method for consistency.

5. **Avoids Duplication**

   - Ensures you're not repeating studies that have already been done.

Steps to Conduct a Literature Review

Step 1: Identify Keywords

- Start with specific terms related to your topic.
- Example: For a study on employee retention, keywords might include "employee turnover," "retention strategies," and "organizational culture."

Step 2: Search for Sources

- Use academic databases like JSTOR, Scopus, Google Scholar, and institutional libraries.
- Look for peer-reviewed journal articles, books, and reports.

Step 3: Evaluate Sources

- Assess each source for credibility, relevance, and recency.
- Example: A study published in a top-tier journal in 2022 is likely more relevant than a non-peer-reviewed article from 2010.

Step 4: Organize Findings

- Group studies by themes, methodologies, or findings.
- Example: Categorize articles on leadership styles into those focusing on transformational, transactional, and laissez-faire leadership.

Step 5: Write the Review

- Summarize the main findings, identify gaps, and connect them to your study.

Example: Literature Review on Leadership Styles

Key Findings:

1. Transformational leadership improves employee engagement (Bass, 1990).
2. Transactional leadership focuses on rewards and performance (Burns, 1978).
3. Few studies explore leadership styles in startups (Gap).

Research Justification: This study will explore how transformational and transactional leadership styles impact employee performance in small startups, addressing the identified gap.

Tools for Conducting Literature Reviews

1. **Zotero and Mendeley**: For managing citations and organizing sources.
2. **NVivo**: For analyzing qualitative data from literature.
3. **Google Scholar Alerts**: To stay updated on new publications related to your topic.
4. **Scopus and Web of Science**: To access high-quality academic journals.

Common Mistakes in Literature Reviews

1. **Using Outdated Sources**

   - Relying on old studies might overlook recent developments. Always prioritize recent work unless foundational theories are required.

2. **Lack of Organization**

   - Jumping between unrelated studies confuses readers. Group similar findings together.

3. **Superficial Summaries**

   ◦ Avoid merely summarizing studies; critically analyze their strengths and weaknesses.

4. **Overlooking Contradictions**

   ◦ Highlight conflicting findings to show where further research is needed.

5. **Not Connecting the Review to Your Study**

   ◦ Clearly state how the literature informs your research problem, objectives, or methods.

Linking theSystematic review of Literature to the Conceptual Framework

The Systematic review of literature provides the foundation for your conceptual framework by identifying key variables, relationships, and theoretical bases.

Example

If previous studies reveal that motivation mediates the effect of leadership style on performance, your conceptual framework could be structured as:
Leadership Style → Motivation → Employee Performance
The review justifies why these variables and relationships are central to your study.

Real-World Application

Case Study: Public Health Research

Topic: Reducing Malnutrition in Rural India

• **Literature Review**: Identifies gaps in understanding the role of community-based initiatives.

   Conceptual Framework:

Community-Based Initiatives → Parental Awareness → Reduction in Malnutrition
Conceptual frameworks and literature reviews are the pillars of rigorous research. While the conceptual framework structures your study, the literature review anchors it in existing knowledge, ensuring relevance and credibility. In the next chapter, we will delve into formulating research objectives and hypotheses—critical components that stem directly from a well-defined problem and framework.

References

Bass, B. M. (1990). *Bass & Stogdill's Handbook of Leadership: Theory, Research, and Managerial Applications*. Free Press.
Burns, J. M. (1978). *Leadership*. Harper & Row.
Creswell, J. W. (2014). *Research design: Qualitative, quantitative, and mixed methods approaches* (4th ed.). Sage Publications.

Kothari, C. R. (2004). *Research methodology: Methods and techniques.* New Age International.

Miles, M. B., & Huberman, A. M. (1994). *Qualitative data analysis: An expanded sourcebook.* Sage Publications.

CHAPTER V

Formulating Research Objectives and Hypotheses

Arjun, a marketing manager, decided to study why his company's e-commerce platform was losing customers. His initial problem statement was clear: **"What factors are causing customer churn?"** However, when asked to present his research objectives, he struggled. He drafted vague goals like "to understand customer behavior" and "to improve retention." His mentor pointed out that without specific objectives, the research would lack focus.

Arjun refined his objectives to:

1. **Determine the impact of website usability on customer satisfaction.**
2. **Assess the role of delivery time in influencing repeat purchases.**
3. **Identify the relationship between price competitiveness and customer loyalty.**

He also formulated hypotheses, such as:

- H_1 : Website usability significantly influences customer satisfaction.
- H_2 : Shorter delivery times lead to higher customer retention.

These focused objectives and hypotheses gave Arjun's research a clear roadmap, ensuring his findings were actionable. This chapter will teach you how to define specific research objectives and formulate testable hypotheses to make your research systematic and effective.

What Are Research Objectives?

Definition

Research objectives are specific statements that outline what the researcher intends to achieve through the study. They provide clarity and direction, breaking down the research problem into actionable parts.

According to Kothari (2004), research objectives are "statements that define the purpose of the research and highlight the issues that the study seeks to address."

Types of Research Objectives

1. **General Objectives**

   - Broad statements outlining the overall aim of the research.
   - Example: To study the factors influencing employee retention in IT firms.

2. **Specific Objectives**

   - Detailed goals focusing on specific aspects of the problem.
   - Example: To examine how workplace flexibility impacts employee retention.

3. **Primary Objectives**

- The core focus of the study, directly linked to the research problem.
- Example: To evaluate the impact of job satisfaction on employee turnover.

4. **Secondary Objectives**

- Additional goals that provide supporting insights or context.
- Example: To analyze the role of demographic factors (age, gender) in employee retention.

Characteristics of Good Research Objectives

1. **Specific and Clear**

- Objectives should be precise and free of ambiguity.
- Example: Instead of "to study employee behavior," write "to analyze the influence of performance appraisals on employee motivation."

2. **Measurable**

- They should define measurable outcomes to assess success.
- Example: "To quantify the percentage increase in customer satisfaction due to improved delivery times."

3. **Achievable**

- Objectives must be realistic, given the available time, resources, and skills.
- Example: Conducting a survey among 500 employees is more achievable than targeting 10,000 participants.

4. **Relevant**

- Objectives should address key aspects of the research problem.
- Example: For a study on remote work, focus on productivity and work-life balance rather than unrelated topics like office design.

5. **Time-Bound**

- Objectives should have a clear timeframe for completion.
- Example: "To analyze the impact of flexible work policies on productivity over a six-month period."

Example of Research Objectives

Research Problem: What factors influence customer loyalty in the e-commerce industry?
  Objectives:

1. To identify the key factors that affect customer loyalty.
2. To analyze the impact of product quality on repeat purchases.
3. To evaluate the role of personalized recommendations in customer satisfaction.

4. To assess the effect of competitive pricing on customer retention.

What Are Hypotheses?

Definition

A hypothesis is a testable prediction of the relationship between two or more variables. It serves as a guide for testing and verifying assumptions through research.

According to Kerlinger (1986), a hypothesis is "a conjectural statement of the relationship between two or more variables."

Purpose of Hypotheses

1. **Provide Direction**

   - Hypotheses focus the study on specific relationships, guiding data collection and analysis.
   - Example: Instead of broadly examining employee satisfaction, a hypothesis could test whether higher salaries improve satisfaction.

2. **Test Relationships**

   - Hypotheses allow researchers to evaluate relationships between variables.
   - Example: Testing whether social media advertising increases brand awareness.

3. **Enable Prediction**

   - Hypotheses predict outcomes, helping researchers anticipate findings.
   - Example: Predicting that shorter delivery times lead to higher customer satisfaction.

4. **Facilitate Statistical Testing**

   - Hypotheses can be tested using statistical methods, ensuring scientific rigor.

Types of Hypotheses

1. **Null Hypothesis (H^0)**

   - Indicates no significant association between variables.
   - Example: H^0: "There is no relationship between workplace flexibility and employee productivity."

2. **Alternative Hypothesis (H_1)**

   - Rejects the null hypothesis and supports the alternative hypothesis.

- Example: H_1 : "Workplace flexibility positively impacts employee productivity."

3. **Directional Hypothesis**

   - Hypothesizes a particular direction for the relationship.
   - Example: "Higher salaries lead to increased job satisfaction."

4. **Non-Directional Hypothesis**

   - Suggests a relationship exists but does not predict its direction.
   - Example: "There is a relationship between job satisfaction and employee turnover."

5. **Complex Hypothesis**

   - Involves multiple independent and dependent variables.
   - Example: "Leadership style and team communication jointly influence employee performance."

Characteristics of Good Hypotheses

1. **Clear and Specific**

   - Hypotheses should be precise and unambiguous.
   - Example: "Customer satisfaction increases with faster delivery times."

2. **Testable**

   - They must be measurable through observation or experimentation.
   - Example: "Offering free returns improves customer loyalty."

3. **Based on Existing Knowledge**

   - Hypotheses should be grounded in prior research or theories.
   - Example: Herzberg's Two-Factor Theory might inspire a hypothesis about job satisfaction.

4. **Logical**

   - Hypotheses should follow logically from the research problem.
   - Example: If the problem is low employee retention, a logical hypothesis might focus on factors like workplace policies or benefits.

5. **Relevant to the Research Problem**

   - Hypotheses should address key aspects of the problem.

Example of Hypotheses

Research Problem: What factors influence e-commerce industry customer loyalty?
   Hypotheses:

- H^0: There is no relationship between product quality and customer loyalty.
- H_1 : Product quality significantly affects customer loyalty.
- H_2 : Competitive pricing positively impacts customer retention.
- H_3 : Personalized recommendations increase repeat purchases.

Linking Research Objectives to Hypotheses

There is close connection between Research Objectives and Hypotheses. Objectives define **what** you want to achieve, while hypotheses predict **how** variables are related.

Example

Objective: To analyze the impact of personalized recommendations on customer satisfaction.
Hypothesis: Personalized recommendations increase customer satisfaction.

Steps to Formulate Research Objectives and Hypotheses

Step 1: Define the Problem Clearly

- A clear problem statement forms the foundation for objectives and hypotheses.
- Example: For employee retention, the problem might be: **"What factors cause high attrition in startups?"**

Step 2: Break Down the Problem

- Divide the problem into specific components.
- Example: Factors like salary, work environment, and leadership style.

Step 3: Set Objectives for Each Component

- Write objectives focusing on each factor.
- Example: "To examine the role of salary in employee retention."

Step 4: Formulate Hypotheses

- Develop testable predictions for each objective.
- Example: "Higher salaries reduce employee turnover."

Step 5: Validate Objectives and Hypotheses

- Ensure they align with the problem and are feasible to test.

Real-World Applications

Case Study: Education Research

Problem: Why are rural students lagging in academic performance?
Objectives:

1. To identify key barriers to academic success in rural schools.
2. To assess the role of teacher training in improving outcomes.

   Hypotheses:

- H_1 : Access to learning materials improves academic performance.
- H_2 : Teacher training programs enhance student outcomes.

Research objectives and hypotheses are essential for guiding your study from start to finish. Objectives define the scope, while hypotheses predict relationships, ensuring your research is focused and actionable. With these tools, you can transform a vague research idea into a systematic, testable study. In the next chapter, we'll explore research designs and how to choose the most suitable one for your objectives and hypotheses.

Basic Issues in Experimental Design

Experimental design is a cornerstone of causal research, allowing researchers to test hypotheses by manipulating variables and observing outcomes. However, designing a robust experiment involves addressing several fundamental issues to ensure validity, reliability, and generalizability.

Key Issues in Experimental Design

1. **Selection of Variables**
   Identifying and categorizing variables is the first step in an experimental design. Variables are typically classified as:

   - **Independent Variable:** The variable that is manipulated (e.g., training programs in an HR study).
   - **Dependent Variable:** The variable that is measured (e.g., employee performance post-training).
   - **Control Variables:** Variables that are kept constant to isolate the effect of the independent variable (e.g., department or job role).
   - **Example in India:** In a study on the impact of rural e-learning programs, the independent variable could be "access to tablets," and the dependent variable could be "student performance."

2. **Control and Randomization**
   Controlling extraneous factors and randomizing subjects are essential to minimize biases and ensure the results are attributable to the independent variable.

   - **Control:** Ensures that other variables do not influence the outcome. For instance, when studying the impact of flexible work policies, factors like team size or job type must be controlled.
   - **Randomization:** Subjects or units are randomly assigned to experimental and control groups, ensuring equal chances of selection.

- **Example:** To test the effectiveness of hybrid learning models in Mumbai schools, students can be randomly assigned to groups using hybrid or traditional methods.

3. **Experimental and Control Groups**
   A well-designed experiment typically involves:

   - **Experimental Group:** Exposed to the independent variable.
   - **Control Group:** Not exposed to the independent variable, serving as a baseline for comparison.
   - **Example in India:** A study on organic fertilizers in Punjab might involve two groups of farmers—one using organic fertilizers and the other using traditional methods.

4. **Threats to Validity**
   Ensuring the validity of experimental results is critical. Validity issues are categorized as:

   - **Internal Validity:** Refers to whether the observed changes in the dependent variable are solely due to the manipulation of the independent variable.

     - **Threats:** Selection bias, history, maturation, and instrumentation changes.

   - **External Validity:** Refers to the generalizability of the findings to other contexts.

     - **Threats:** Sample representativeness and artificiality of the experimental setting.

   - **Example:** An internal validity threat could arise if a study on workplace productivity during remote work also coincides with a major company policy change.

5. **Blinding and Placebos**

   - **Single-Blind Study:** Participants are unaware of the experimental conditions they are in, reducing response bias.
   - **Double-Blind Study:** Both participants and researchers are unaware of group assignments, eliminating researcher bias.
   - **Placebos:** Used in fields like healthcare research to create a baseline for comparison.
   - **Example:** In a pharmaceutical study in Bengaluru, researchers might use a placebo to test the effectiveness of a new diabetes medication.

6. **Replication and Reliability**
   Experiments must be replicable to ensure reliability. Other researchers should achieve similar results under similar conditions. These builds trust in the findings and supports their application in other contexts.

   - **Example:** A pilot study on cashless payment systems in Kerala can be replicated in another state to validate its conclusions.

7. **Ethical Considerations**

   - Ethical practices ensure that participants' rights and safety are protected during the experiment.
   - Informed consent, confidentiality, and minimizing harm are critical ethical principles.

- **Example:** A study on mental health interventions for college students in Delhi must ensure anonymity and voluntary participation.

Real-World Applications in India

1. **Education Research:**
   An experimental study in Rajasthan might test whether the introduction of gamified learning apps improves academic performance compared to traditional teaching methods.
2. **Agriculture Studies:**
   A study in Maharashtra could examine whether organic fertilizers improve crop yield compared to chemical fertilizers, using experimental and control groups.
3. **E-Commerce Experiments:**
   Flipkart could conduct A/B testing on their website to evaluate whether personalized recommendations improve sales conversions.

Addressing the basic issues in experimental design ensures that research findings are credible and actionable. By carefully selecting variables, controlling extraneous factors, and addressing validity concerns, researchers can design experiments that generate meaningful insights. In Indian contexts, such designs play a vital role in policy-making, product innovation, and social development.

References

Creswell, J. W. (2014). *Research design: Qualitative, quantitative, and mixed methods approaches* (4th ed.). Sage Publications.
Kerlinger, F. N. (1986). *Foundations of behavioral research.* Holt, Rinehart, and Winston.
Kothari, C. R. (2004). *Research methodology: Methods and techniques.* New Age International.
Neuman, W. L. (2014). *Social research methods: Qualitative and quantitative approaches* (7th ed.). Pearson Education.

CHAPTER VI

Research Design and Methodology

Meera, an HR consultant, was tasked with studying the effect of remote work policies on employee productivity. Excited to begin, she started interviewing employees and analyzing their feedback. But soon, her mentor pointed out that her approach lacked structure. She hadn't decided **how** to conduct the research—should it be a survey, an experiment, or a case study? She also hadn't considered her sampling method or data collection tools.

Meera realized she needed a **research design**, a detailed plan that would serve as a blueprint for her study. Once she designed a framework that outlined her objectives, methods, and data analysis strategies, her research became focused and efficient.

This chapter delves into the importance of research design and methodology, discussing their types, components, and applications in social sciences and management.

What is a Research Design?

Definition

A research design is a comprehensive and systematic plan that guides the entire research process. It encompasses the overall strategy for addressing the research problem, including:

- **Clearly defined research objectives and hypotheses:** These outline what the study aims to achieve and the specific predictions to be tested.
- **Choice of research methodology:** This involves selecting the appropriate research approach (e.g., experimental, survey, qualitative) based on the research question and objectives.
- **Data collection methods:** This includes specifying the techniques used to gather data, such as surveys, interviews, observations, experiments, or document analysis.
- **Sampling procedures:** This determines how participants or data sources will be selected to ensure representativeness and minimize bias.
- **Data analysis plan:** This outlines the statistical or qualitative methods that will be used to analyze the collected data and draw meaningful conclusions.
- **Ethical considerations:** This addresses the ethical implications of the research and ensures that it is conducted in a responsible and ethical manner.

In essence, a well-crafted research design acts as a roadmap, ensuring that the research is conducted efficiently, effectively, and with a high degree of validity and reliability. It provides a clear framework for the entire research process, from the initial conceptualization to the final interpretation of resculls.

Creswell (2014) defines a research design as "a plan or proposal to conduct research that involves the intersection of philosophy, strategies of inquiry, and specific methods."

Importance of Research Design

1. **Provides Structure to Research**

   - A well-defined design assures that the study follows a sequential logic, from identifying the problem to interpreting results.

- Example: In a study on employee engagement, the design helps clarify whether to use surveys, interviews, or both.

2. **Enhances Validity and Reliability**

   - A good design minimizes errors and biases, ensuring credible results.
   - Example: Randomized sampling improves the validity of findings in social science research.

3. **Efficient Resource Management**

   - It ensures optimal use of time, funds, and manpower.
   - Example: A cross-sectional survey is more cost-effective than a longitudinal study for short-term goals.

4. **Aligns Methods with Objectives**

   - The design ensures that the methods used for data collection and analysis are closely aligned with the research goals.
   - Example: A study examining cause-and-effect relationships may use an experimental design.

5. **Facilitates Comparability**

   A well-structured design facilitates the replication of results and comparison across similar studies.

Types of Research Design

Research designs are broadly classified into three types: **exploratory**, **descriptive**, and **causal**.

1. Exploratory Research Design

- **Definition**: Used when knowledge is limited about a topic, and the aim is to explore and generate ideas or hypotheses.
- **Example in Social Sciences**: A study exploring why rural communities resist government vaccination programs.
- **Methods Used**:

  - Literature reviews.
  - Focus groups.
  - Open-ended interviews.

- **Strengths**:

  - Provides insights into unexplored areas.
  - Flexible and adaptable to emerging findings.

- **Limitations**:

  - Cannot establish causality or test hypotheses.

2. Descriptive Research Design

- **Definition**: Focuses on systematically describing a phenomenon or group characteristics without examining cause-and-effect relationships.
- **Example in Management**: A survey measuring job satisfaction among employees in IT firms.
- **Methods Used**:

  - Structured surveys.
  - Observational studies.
  - Case studies.

- **Strengths**:

  - Provides detailed, quantitative, or qualitative descriptions.
  - Helps identify patterns and trends.

- **Limitations**:

  - Does not explain why phenomena occur.

3. *Causal Research Design*

- **Definition**: Examines cause-and-effect relationships by testing hypotheses.
- **Example in Management**: An experiment studying whether flexible work hours improve employee productivity.
- **Methods Used**:

  - Experiments.
  - Quasi-experiments.
  - Statistical modeling.

- **Strengths**:

  - Establishes causality.
  - Generates actionable insights.

- **Limitations**:

  - Requires rigorous control of variables, which can be challenging.

Key Components of Research Design

1. **Research Objectives**

   - It defines the general direction and intended achievements of the research.

- Example: "To analyze the impact of training programs on employee retention."

2. **Data Collection Methods**

  - Choose from a wide range of techniques, including surveys, interviews, experiments, and observations.
  - Example: For customer satisfaction, use structured questionnaires with Likert scales.

3. **Sampling Techniques**

  - Decide how participants or data sources will be selected.
  - Example:Random sampling ensures that every individual in the population has an equal and independent chance of being selected for the sample.

4. **Tools and Instruments**

  - Specify tools like software, recording devices, or measurement scales.
  - Example: SPSS for statistical analysis or NVivo for qualitative data coding.

5. **Data Analysis Plan**

  - Define how data will be processed and interpreted.
  - Example: Using regression analysis to test hypotheses about employee performance.

6. **Ethical Considerations**

  - Address issues like informed consent, confidentiality, and participant safety.

Categories of Exploratory Research

Exploratory research aims to investigate an uncharted area or problem, uncovering patterns, ideas, or hypotheses that may not be immediately apparent. While exploratory research is flexible and broad in nature, it is often categorized based on the methods used to gather insights.

1. Literature Review

A literature review is one of the most common methods in exploratory research. It involves analyzing existing studies, reports, and theoretical frameworks to identify gaps or patterns that inform future research.

- **Application Example in India:**

  - An e-commerce platform like Amazon India might review academic studies and market reports on rural online shopping habits to identify untapped customer segments.

- **Strengths:**

  - Provides a broad understanding of the research landscape.
  - Helps in framing research questions.

- **Limitations:**

  - Relies on existing information and may overlook new or emerging phenomena.

2. Focus Groups

Focus groups gather insights through moderated discussions among small, diverse groups of participants. This method is highly effective in generating a wide range of opinions and exploring ideas in depth.

- **Application Example in India:**

  - Flipkart could conduct focus groups in semi-urban areas to understand barriers to online shopping adoption.

- **Strengths:**

  - Facilitates interactive discussions that reveal hidden perspectives.
  - Allows participants to build on each other's ideas.

- **Limitations:**

  - Group dynamics may suppress individual opinions.
  - Not suitable for sensitive topics.

3. Expert Interviews

Exploratory research often relies on interviews with subject matter experts to gain in-depth knowledge about a topic. These interviews can provide valuable insights into emerging trends or challenges.

- **Application Example in India:**

  - Consulting firms like McKinsey India may interview healthcare experts to explore opportunities in telemedicine.

- **Strengths:**

  - Offers detailed insights from experienced professionals.
  - Helps refine research focus.

- **Limitations:**

  - Opinions may be subjective and not fully representative.

4. Case Studies

Case studies involve the detailed examination of a specific individual, group, event, or organization to uncover broader insights.

- **Application Example in India:**

  - A case study on the adoption of renewable energy by Tata Power could provide insights into best practices for other companies in the sector.

- **Strengths:**

- Provides a rich, contextual understanding of the subject.
- Generates practical examples for future research.

- **Limitations:**

  - Findings may not be generalizable.

5. Observational Studies

This method involves observing behaviors or phenomena in their natural setting without direct interference. Observational studies are particularly useful for understanding human interactions, processes, or environmental conditions.

- **Application Example in India:**

  - Observing customer behavior in Big Bazaar stores can help understand shopping patterns and preferences.

- **Strengths:**

  - Captures real-world behavior.
  - Useful when participants may not articulate their preferences clearly.

- **Limitations:**

  - Observer bias can influence data interpretation.
  - Limited control over external variables.

6. Pilot Studies

Pilot studies are small-scale preliminary studies conducted to test the feasibility of a larger research project. They are commonly used to refine methodologies or test hypotheses.

- **Application Example in India:**

  - A pilot study on electric vehicle adoption in Bengaluru could help policymakers design a larger-scale initiative.

- **Strengths:**

  - Identifies potential issues before full-scale research.
  - Reduces risks associated with large projects.

- **Limitations:**

  - Findings may not always scale to larger populations.

Exploratory research provides the foundation for more structured studies by uncovering patterns, generating hypotheses, and identifying gaps. In the Indian context, exploratory research has been pivotal in understanding diverse markets, customer behaviors, and social challenges. By utilizing a mix of methods such as focus groups, case studies, and observational studies, researchers can gain valuable insights to guide future research endeavors.

Research Methodology

Definition

Research methodology is the blueprint for conducting research. It outlines the step-by-step process, including the rationale for chosen methods and techniques, ensuring a clear, logical, and reproducible investigation.

Importance of Methodology

1. **Ensures Systematic Inquiry**

   ◦ A sound methodology guarantees that research is conducted logically and consistently.

2. **Improves Accuracy**

   ◦ Using appropriate techniques reduces the risk of errors.

3. **Facilitates Replication**

   ◦ Clearly defined methods allow other researchers to replicate the study.

Types of Research Methodologies

1. Qualitative Methodology

- Focuses on non-numeric data like text, images, or videos.
- Example: Using interviews to understand employee experiences with remote work.
- **Tools:** NVivo, thematic analysis.

2. Quantitative Methodology

- Focuses on collecting and analyzing numerical data to identify patterns, trends, and causal relationships. It employs statistical methods to measure variables, test hypotheses, and draw inferences about larger populations.
- Example: Analyzing survey responses to measure customer satisfaction.
- **Tools:** SPSS, Excel, R.

3. Mixed-Methods Methodology

- Combines qualitative and quantitative techniques for comprehensive insights.
- Example: Conducting surveys (quantitative) and focus groups (qualitative) to study employee engagement.

Real-World Example: Research Design in Action

Topic: Improving Student Performance in Rural Schools

1. **Objectives**:

   - To identify barriers to academic success.
   - To evaluate the impact of teacher training programs.

2. **Design**:

   - **Type**: Descriptive research.
   - **Data Collection**: Surveys for students and interviews with teachers.
   - **Sampling**: Stratified sampling of schools in different regions.

3. **Methodology**:

   - Mixed-methods approach.
   - Quantitative surveys to measure student performance metrics.
   - Qualitative interviews to understand teacher challenges.

Common Mistakes in Research Design and Methodology

1. **Overly Broad Design**

   - Trying to study too many variables leads to unfocused research.
   - Solution: Narrow down the scope to a manageable number of objectives.

2. **Poor Sampling Techniques**

   - Using non-representative samples skews results.
   - Solution: Employ probability sampling techniques for generalizable findings.

3. **Mismatched Methods**

   - Choosing methods that don't align with research objectives.
   - Solution: Ensure methods are suited to the study's goals (e.g., experiments for causality).

4. **Ignoring Ethical Considerations**

   - Failing to obtain informed consent can lead to ethical violations.
   - Solution: Follow guidelines like those from the American Psychological Association (APA).

A well-designed research framework is the backbone of successful studies. By choosing the appropriate design and research methods, researchers can assure their findings are accurate, reliable, and relevant. Whether it is exploratory, descriptive, or causal, aligning the research design with objectives is essential for meaningful outcomes. In the next chapter, we'll explore sampling techniques and strategies for collecting high-quality data.

References

Creswell, J. W. (2014). *Research design: Qualitative, quantitative, and mixed methods approaches* (4th ed.). Sage Publications.

Kothari, C. R. (2004). *Research methodology: Methods and techniques.* New Age International.

Neuman, W. L. (2014). *Social research methods: Qualitative and quantitative approaches* (7th ed.). Pearson Education.

Robson, C. (2007). *How to do a research project: A guide for undergraduate students.* Blackwell Publishing.

CHAPTER VII

Sampling Techniques and Data Collection Methods

Ravi, a marketing researcher, wanted to study consumer preferences for electric vehicles (EVs) in India. Excited to collect data, he decided to survey a group of 50 friends and family. After presenting his findings to his supervisor, he was met with a simple question: **"How representative is your sample of the entire EV market?"**

Ravi realized that his data didn't reflect the broader population—his sample was biased toward urban, tech-savvy individuals. His supervisor introduced him to the concept of **sampling techniques**, explaining how a well-chosen sample could yield results that are valid for the entire population. With this guidance, Ravi restructured his study, using stratified random sampling to include participants from various demographics, regions, and income levels.

This chapter will guide you through the significance of sampling and data collection, exploring various methods and emphasizing the importance of data quality and reliability in your research.

What is Sampling?

Definition

Sampling is the process of choosing a representative sample from a larger population with the aim of making inferences about the characteristics of the entire population based on the analysis of the selected subset.

As per Kothari (2004), sampling is "the selection of some part of an aggregate or totality on the basis of which a judgment or inference about the aggregate or totality is made."

Importance of Sampling

1. **Saves Time and Resources**

   - Studying a smaller, well-chosen sample is quicker and more cost-effective than analyzing an entire population.
   - Example: Instead of surveying every commuter in a city, researchers can analyze a representative sample to understand public transport usage.

2. **Enables Feasibility**

   - Sampling makes large-scale studies manageable, especially when populations are vast.
   - Example: Conducting a nationwide study on EV adoption requires sampling, as surveying the entire country is impractical.

3. **Improves Accuracy**

   - A carefully selected sample can yield results that closely approximate those of the population.
   - Example: A sample of 1,000 diverse respondents might provide reliable insights into voter behavior.

4. **Allows for Generalization**

   - With proper sampling techniques, researchers can generalize findings to the broader population.

5. Ensures Statistical Significance

- Sampling provides the basis for applying statistical tests and validating hypotheses.

Types of Sampling Techniques

Sampling techniques can be broadly classified into two broad categoriess:Random Sampling Techniques (based on **probability sampling)** and Non-Random Sampling Techniques (not based on **probability sampling).**

1. Probability Sampling

Probability sampling ensures that each member of the population has an equal opportunity of being selected, promoting representativeness, and minimizing bias.

a. Simple Random Sampling

- **Definition**: Chances of selection of each and every member are equal.
- **Example**: Drawing random names from a database of 10,000 customers.
- **Advantages**: Unbiased and easy to implement.
- **Disadvantages**: Relies on having a comprehensive and up-to-date list of the entire population, which may not always be readily available.

b. Stratified Sampling

- **Definition:** Stratified sampling is a probability sampling technique that divides the population into distinct subgroups or strata based on shared characteristics. Samples are then randomly selected from each stratum to ensure representation of all subgroups within the population.
- **Example**: Surveying urban and rural consumers separately to study EV preferences.
- **Advantages**: Ensures representation of all key groups.
- **Disadvantages**: More complex and time-consuming.

c. Cluster Sampling

- **Definition: Cluster sampling** is a probability sampling method where the population is divided into naturally occurring, **internally heterogeneous but externally homogeneous** groups called clusters. The population is divided into clusters, and a few clusters are randomly selected for study.
- **Example**: Selecting specific districts in a state to study agricultural practices.
- **Advantages**: Cost-effective for geographically dispersed populations.
- **Disadvantages**: Results may be less precise if clusters are not homogeneous.

d. Systematic Sampling

- **Definition**: Every nth member of the population is selected.
- **Example**: Selecting every 10ᵗʰ passenger in a train station to study commuting habits.
- **Advantages**: Easy to implement.
- **Disadvantages**: Can introduce bias if the population order follows a pattern.

2. Non-Probability Sampling

In non-probability sampling, the selection is based on subjective judgment rather than randomization. While less representative, it is useful for exploratory research.

a. Convenience Sampling

- **Definition**: Participants are chosen based on their availability or convenience.
- **Example**: Interviewing shoppers at a nearby mall to understand consumer behavior.
- **Advantages**: Quick and inexpensive.
- **Disadvantages**: Highly prone to bias and not generalizable.

b. Purposive Sampling

- **Definition**: Participants are selected based on specific criteria relevant to the study.
- **Example**: Studying only farmers with access to government subsidies.
- **Advantages**: Focused on the target population.
- **Disadvantages**: Subjective and potentially biased.

c. Snowball Sampling

- **Definition**: Existing participants recruit others, creating a chain referral process.
- **Example**: Studying a niche group, like freelancers, where initial participants refer their peers.
- **Advantages**: Useful for hard-to-reach populations.
- **Disadvantages**: Non-random and potentially biased.

d. Quota Sampling

- **Definition**: Researchers ensure specific quotas (e.g., 50% males, 50% females) are filled in the sample.
- **Example**: Ensuring equal representation of genders in a survey on workplace diversity.
- **Advantages**: Guarantees subgroup representation.
- **Disadvantages**: May introduce selection bias.

Determination of Sample Size

Determining the appropriate sample size is a crucial step in any research study. The sample size directly impacts the reliability, validity, and generalizability of the findings. An inadequately small sample may lead to unreliable conclusions, while an excessively large sample could waste resources without additional benefits.

Factors Influencing Sample Size

1. **Research Objectives:**
   The scope and complexity of the study dictate the sample size. For example, a study aiming to generalize findings across India will require a larger sample than one focused on a single city.
2. **Population Size (N):**
   The total number of elements in the population impacts sample size determination. In smaller populations, researchers often require a larger proportion of the population to ensure representativeness.

- ◦ **Example in India:**
  A study of tribal artisans in Odisha may involve a smaller population compared to urban e-commerce shoppers.

3. **Margin of Error (E):**
   This is the maximum allowable difference between the sample estimate and the true population value. A smaller margin of error requires a larger sample size.

   - ◦ Typical Values: ±5% for general studies, ±3% for precise results.

4. **Confidence Level (Z):**
   The confidence level indicates the probability that the sample accurately reflects the population. Commonly used values are 90%, 95%, and 99%, with 95% being the most standard.

   - ◦ **Z-Scores:**

     - 90% Confidence Level: Z = 1.645
     - 95% Confidence Level: Z = 1.96
     - 99% Confidence Level: Z = 2.576

5. **Variability in the Population (P):**
   The greater the variability in the population, the larger the sample size required. When population variability is unknown, researchers often use P = 0.5 for maximum variability.
6. **Type of Study:**
   Quantitative studies typically require larger sample sizes than qualitative studies to achieve statistical significance.

   - ◦ **Example in India:**
     A survey measuring customer satisfaction at Flipkart would require more respondents compared to an exploratory study on shopping behaviors.

Sample Size Calculation Formula
For large populations, researchers use the following formula:

$$n = \frac{Z^2 \cdot P \cdot (1 - P)}{E^2}$$

Where:

- **n** = Required sample size
- **Z** = Z-score corresponding to the confidence level
- **P** = Proportion of the population (expressed as a decimal, e.g., 0.5)
- **E** = Margin of error (expressed as a decimal, e.g., 0.05 for 5%)

Adjusting for Finite Populations
When the population size (N) is finite, the formula is adjusted as follows:

The adjusted sample size (n_{finite}) is calculated using the formula:

$$n_{\text{finite}} = \frac{n}{1 + \frac{n-1}{N}}$$

Where:

- **N** = Population size

Practical Example: Calculating Sample Size

- **Scenario:**
A researcher wants to study online shopping behavior among customers in Mumbai.

  - Population size (N): 10,000
  - Confidence level: 95% (Z = 1.96)
  - Variability (P): 0.5
  - Margin of error (E): 5% (0.05)

- **Step 1: Calculate Initial Sample Size (n):**

The formula for calculating the sample size is:

$$n = \frac{Z^2 \cdot P \cdot (1 - P)}{E^2}$$

Where:

- $Z = 1.96$ (Z-score for a 95% confidence level)

- $P = 0.5$ (proportion of the population, assuming maximum variability)

- $E = 0.05$ (margin of error)

Substitute the values into the formula:

$$n = \frac{1.96^2 \cdot 0.5 \cdot (1 - 0.5)}{0.05^2}$$

$$n = \frac{3.8416 \cdot 0.25}{0.0025}$$

$$n = \frac{0.9604}{0.0025}$$

$$n = 384.16$$

- **Step 2: Adjust for Finite Population (n_finite):**

The formula for adjusting the sample size for a finite population is:

$$n_{\text{finite}} = \frac{n}{1 + \frac{n-1}{N}}$$

Where:

- $n = 384.16$ (initial sample size calculated in Step 1)
- $N = 10,000$ (total population size)

Substitute the values into the formula:

$$n_{\text{finite}} = \frac{384.16}{1 + \frac{384.16 - 1}{10,000}}$$

$$n_{\text{finite}} = \frac{384.16}{1 + \frac{383.16}{10,000}}$$

$$n_{\text{finite}} = \frac{384.16}{1 + 0.038316}$$

$$n_{\text{finite}} = \frac{384.16}{1.038316}$$

$$n_{\text{finite}} \approx 370$$

Thus, the required sample size is approximately **370 respondents**

Practical Guidelines for Sample Size

1. **Small Population (<500):** Use a higher proportion of the population to ensure representation.
2. **Moderate Population (500–10,000):** Adjust sample size using the finite population formula.
3. **Large Population (>10,000):** The initial formula without adjustment often suffices.

Real-World Applications in India

1. **Elections:**
   Polling agencies like Lokniti-CSDS use sample size formulas to determine the number of respondents required for pre-election surveys.
2. **Healthcare:**
   A study on vaccination rates in rural Bihar might require precise sampling to account for variability in socio-economic factors.
3. **Retail Research:**
   Companies like Reliance Retail calculate optimal sample sizes to test customer satisfaction in their stores across India.

Determining the right sample size is critical for ensuring the accuracy, reliability, and validity of research findings. By considering factors like population size, confidence level, and variability, researchers can design studies that are both cost-effective and representative. Proper sample size determination is particularly important in India, where diverse and heterogeneous populations require careful planning to ensure meaningful results.

Data Collection Methods

Data collection is the process of gathering information to address the research problem. It can involve primary or secondary sources, depending on the research objectives.

1. Primary Data Collection

Primary data is collected firsthand for the specific research purpose.

a. Surveys

- **Definition**: Structured questionnaires distributed to participants.
- **Example**: Surveying 1,000 respondents on online shopping preferences.
- **Advantages**: Collects data from large groups quickly.
- **Disadvantages**: Risk of low response rates or poorly designed questions.

b. Interviews

- **Definition**: One-on-one conversations to gather in-depth insights.
- **Example**: Interviewing rural women to understand their challenges in accessing microfinance.
- **Advantages**: Provides rich, detailed data.
- **Disadvantages**: Time-consuming and prone to interviewer bias.

c. Focus Groups

- **Definition**: Group discussions led by a moderator to explore participant opinions.
- **Example**: Discussing customer satisfaction with a panel of regular shoppers.
- **Advantages**: Encourages dynamic discussions.
- **Disadvantages**: Group dynamics can suppress individual opinions.

d. Observation

- **Definition**: Watching and recording behaviors in a natural setting.
- **Example**: Observing buying patterns in a supermarket.
- **Advantages**: Captures authentic behaviors.
- **Disadvantages**: Observer bias and limited scope.

2. Secondary Data Collection

Secondary data is collected from existing sources, such as reports, articles, and databases.

a. Government Reports

- Example: Census data used to study migration trends.
- **Advantages**: Reliable and comprehensive.
- **Disadvantages**: May not address specific research needs.

b. Industry Reports

- Example: Market analysis reports on consumer preferences for smartphones.
- **Advantages**: Offers detailed insights into industry trends.

- **Disadvantages**: Often expensive and proprietary.

   c. Academic Literature

- Example: Journals and books used to study theories and models.
- **Advantages**: High-quality and peer-reviewed.
- **Disadvantages**: Can be time-consuming to analyze.

Common Mistakes in Sampling and Data Collection

1. **Biased Sampling**

   - Over-representing certain groups while neglecting others.
   - Solution: Use probability sampling techniques for representativeness.

2. **Poorly Designed Instruments**

   - Ambiguous survey questions or inconsistent interview guides can lead to unreliable data.
   - Solution: Pilot-test instruments before full deployment.

3. **Insufficient Sample Size**

   - A small sample reduces the statistical power of the study.
   - Solution: Calculate the required sample size based on population characteristics.

4. **Ignoring Ethical Issues**

   - Collecting data without informed consent or violating privacy.
   - Solution: Adhere to ethical guidelines and secure participant consent.

Real-World Application

Case Study: Studying Urban Commuter Preferences

Research Problem: Why are commuters reluctant to use public buses in urban areas?

1. **Sampling**: Stratified sampling to include commuters from different income levels, genders, and age groups.
2. **Data Collection**:

   - Surveys to measure satisfaction with bus services.
   - Observations at bus stops to record waiting times and crowding.
   - Interviews with regular commuters to understand pain points.

   This mixed-methods approach ensures comprehensive insights.

Sampling techniques and data collection methods are the backbone of any research study. By selecting an appropriate sample and using reliable data collection methods, researchers can ensure their findings are representative, valid, and actionable. The next chapter will delve into data analysis techniques, exploring how to process and interpret the data collected during research.

References

Creswell, J. W. (2014). *Research design: Qualitative, quantitative, and mixed methods approaches* (4th ed.). Sage Publications.
Kothari, C. R. (2004). *Research methodology: Methods and techniques*. New Age International.
Neuman, W. L. (2014). *Social research methods: Qualitative and quantitative approaches* (7th ed.). Pearson Education.
Robson, C. (2007). *How to do a research project: A guide for undergraduate students*. Blackwell Publishing.

CHAPTER VIII

Data Analysis and Interpretation

Tara, a graduate student in management, conducted a survey on employee job satisfaction across different industries. She collected responses from 500 employees, entered the data into Excel, and stared at the sheet, overwhelmed by the rows of numbers. Her mentor asked, "What's your plan for analyzing this data?" Tara realized she hadn't thought about data analysis—how to identify patterns, compare responses, or test her hypotheses.

Her mentor explained the importance of structured data analysis techniques and the rationale for choosing specific tools and methods. Tara systematically learned how to clean the data, apply descriptive and inferential statistics, and interpret results. With proper analysis, she uncovered that employees valued flexibility over salary increments, helping her suggest actionable HR policies.

This chapter will make you an expert in data analysis by delving into every method with practical examples, explaining **when and why** each tool is appropriate, **how to apply it**, and **what its limitations are**.

What is Data Analysis?

Definition

Data analysis is the process of examining, organizing, and interpreting raw data to uncover patterns, test hypotheses, and derive actionable insights. It includes a range of logical and statistical techniques to make sense of complex datasets.

For example, a researcher studying consumer behavior may analyze survey responses to determine why customers prefer online shopping over in-store shopping. According to Neuman (2014), "Data analysis is the process of systematically searching for patterns and arranging data to provide explanations, support decisions, and expand understanding."

Importance of Data Analysis

1. **Transforms Raw Data into Insights**
   Raw data is unstructured and difficult to interpret. Through analysis, researchers identify meaningful patterns and summarize results. For example, analyzing survey data about customer loyalty can reveal that personalized discounts increase retention rates. Without analysis, this insight would remain hidden.
2. **Validates Hypotheses**
   Data analysis confirms or rejects the hypotheses formulated during the research process. For example, if a researcher hypothesizes that remote work improves productivity, data analysis tools like regression can test whether the hypothesis holds true. This is critical for evidence-based conclusions.
3. **Supports Decision-Making**
   Governments, businesses, and organizations rely on data analysis to make strategic decisions. For instance, analyzing healthcare data may reveal gaps in vaccine coverage, prompting targeted interventions. Without this information, resources may be misallocated.
4. **Ensures Credibility**
   Reliable and systematic analysis enhances the validity of research findings. Studies with robust analysis gain credibility among stakeholders, leading to broader acceptance and use of the findings.

5. **Simplifies Complexity**

   Complex datasets with thousands of variables can overwhelm researchers. Analytical tools like statistical summaries, charts, and graphs make such data comprehensible. For instance, visualizing income disparities using a bar graph simplifies the interpretation of economic inequality.

Descriptive and Inferential Statistics

Data analysis in research involves two primary approaches: **descriptive statistics** and **inferential statistics**. While descriptive statistics summarize and describe the data, inferential statistics help researchers make predictions or draw conclusions about a population based on a sample.

1. Descriptive Statistics

Descriptive statistics provide a snapshot of the dataset by summarizing its main features. They focus on presenting data in a clear and understandable manner, often through visual tools like graphs and charts.

Key Components of Descriptive Statistics:

1. **Measures of Central Tendency:**

   These indicate the average or most common values in the dataset.

   - **Mean:** The arithmetic average.
   - **Median:** The middle value when data is arranged in order.
   - **Mode:** The most frequently occurring value.
   - **Example in India:**
     A study on household income in Delhi might report the mean monthly income as ₹50,000, with a median of ₹ 45,000.

2. **Measures of Dispersion:**

   These describe the variability or spread of data.

   - **Range:** The difference between the highest and lowest values.
   - **Variance:** The average squared deviation from the mean.
   - **Standard Deviation:** The square root of variance, showing how spread out the values are.
   - **Example in India:**
     Analyzing the standard deviation of smartphone prices in the Indian market to assess price variation.

3. **Frequency Distributions:**

   Frequency tables and histograms display how often different values occur.

   - **Example:**
     A frequency distribution of voting patterns across Indian states.

4. **Visual Representations:**

   Charts, graphs, and tables simplify data interpretation.

   - **Example:**
     Pie charts depicting the percentage share of different sectors in India's GDP.

   2. Inferential Statistics

Inferential statistics allow researchers to generalize findings from a sample to the larger population. They are used to test hypotheses, estimate population parameters, and identify relationships between variables.

Key Techniques in Inferential Statistics:

1. **Estimation:**
Estimation involves determining population parameters (e.g., mean or proportion) using sample data.

   - **Point Estimate:** A single value estimate (e.g., sample mean).
   - **Confidence Interval:** A range within which the population parameter likely falls.
   - **Example in India:**
     Estimating the percentage of rural households with access to clean drinking water.

2. **Hypothesis Testing:**
Hypothesis testing evaluates whether a claim about a population parameter is supported by sample data. It involves:

   - Null Hypothesis (H^0): Assumes no effect or relationship.
   - Alternative Hypothesis (H_1): Suggests a significant effect or relationship.

Common tests include:

   - **t-tests:** Compare means between two groups.
   - **ANOVA:** Analyze differences between multiple groups.
   - **Chi-Square Test:** Assess relationships between categorical variables.
   - **Example in India:**
     A t-test to compare literacy rates between rural and urban areas.

2. **Regression Analysis:**
Regression identifies relationships between dependent and independent variables.

   - **Linear Regression:** Examines how one variable predicts another.
   - **Multiple Regression:** Involves multiple predictors.
   - **Example in India:**
     Using regression to analyze the impact of marketing expenditure on sales revenue for a company like Dabur.

3. **Correlation Analysis:**
Measures the strength and direction of the relationship between two variables.

   - **Pearson Correlation Coefficient (r):** Values range from -1 (perfect negative) to +1 (perfect positive).
   - **Example:**
     Correlation between rainfall levels and crop yields in Maharashtra.

4. **Sampling Distributions and Standard Error:**
Inferential statistics use sampling distributions to estimate how sample statistics (e.g., sample mean) vary across different samples.

   - **Standard Error:** Indicates the accuracy of a sample statistic as an estimate of the population parameter.

- ○ **Example in India:**
  Calculating the standard error when estimating the average monthly income of IT professionals in Bengaluru.

Key Differences Between Descriptive and Inferential Statistics

Aspect	Descriptive Statistics	Inferential Statistics
Purpose	Summarizes and describes data.	Draws conclusions about a population from sample data.
Tools Used	Measures of central tendency, dispersion, and visualization.	Hypothesis testing, confidence intervals, regression.
Scope	Limited to the dataset at hand.	Generalizes findings to the broader population.
Example Application	Calculating average customer age in a mall survey.	Estimating the average customer age in the entire city.

Real-World Applications in India

1. **Government Policy Analysis:**
   Descriptive statistics help analyze census data, while inferential statistics predict trends like urban migration.
2. **Healthcare Research:**
   Inferential statistics are used in clinical trials to test the effectiveness of new treatments or drugs.
3. **Market Research:**
   Descriptive statistics summarize customer preferences, while inferential statistics predict future purchasing behaviors.

Descriptive and inferential statistics are complementary tools that enable researchers to summarize data effectively and draw meaningful conclusions. While descriptive statistics provide insights into the data at hand, inferential statistics extend these findings to broader populations, making them indispensable in decision-making and strategic planning.

Types of Data Analysis

Data analysis is broadly categorized into **qualitative** (non-numeric) and **quantitative** (numeric) approaches.

1. Qualitative Data Analysis

Qualitative analysis focuses on non-numeric data, such as interview transcripts, images, or open-ended survey responses. This approach is exploratory and seeks to understand experiences, behaviors, or phenomena in depth. It is particularly useful for answering "why" or "how" questions.

Methods of Qualitative Analysis

A. **Thematic Analysis**

Thematic analysis is one of the most widely used techniques in qualitative research to identify, analyze, and report patterns (or themes) within data. A "theme" represents significant ideas or recurring concepts that provide meaningful insights into a particular topic or phenomenon. Researchers use thematic analysis to distill large amounts of qualitative data, such as interview transcripts or focus group discussions, into manageable and interpretable results by identifying commonalities across the dataset. This method is particularly effective for exploring unstructured or complex data where predefined variables are unavailable.

How Thematic Analysis Works

Thematic analysis typically begins with the researcher familiarizing themselves with the raw data by reading and re-reading transcripts, open-ended survey responses, or other qualitative inputs. This step helps them develop an initial understanding of the information and context. Next, the data is coded, where specific words, phrases, or sections of text are assigned short labels that summarize their content. For example, in interviews about workplace culture, statements like "I can speak freely in team meetings" might be coded as "open communication."

The researcher then groups similar codes to form broader themes. These themes represent patterns that are repeated across the dataset, such as "team collaboration," "employee satisfaction," or "supportive environment." For instance, codes such as "open communication" and "mutual respect" might be grouped into a larger theme like "supportive environment." This process requires iterative refinement, as themes are reviewed, modified, and sometimes combined to ensure they capture the dataset's essence.

Practical Example

Consider a qualitative study exploring customer feedback about a new mobile app. The researcher begins by coding phrases like "easy to navigate," "intuitive design," and "great user interface." These codes can later be grouped under the theme "user-friendly design." Similarly, complaints like "app crashes frequently" and "slow loading times" might contribute to a theme called "technical issues." By analyzing these themes, the researcher can identify areas for improvement and potential strengths to highlight in future marketing efforts.

When to Use Thematic Analysis

Thematic analysis is particularly useful in exploratory research, where researchers aim to gain insights into a topic without predefined hypotheses or categories. It is an ideal method for studies seeking to understand subjective experiences, behaviors, or attitudes. For instance, researchers investigating employee morale might use thematic analysis to uncover the underlying reasons for dissatisfaction, such as "lack of recognition" or "poor work-life balance."

It is also widely applicable in studies focusing on customer opinions, societal trends, educational practices, healthcare experiences, or any domain where participants' perspectives play a central role.

Steps to Apply Thematic Analysis

1. **Familiarize Yourself with the Data**: Carefully read through all the data, such as interview transcripts or open-ended survey responses, and take notes on initial impressions.
2. **Generate Initial Codes**: Break down the data into smaller chunks and assign descriptive labels (codes) to key words, phrases, or segments. For example, if a participant says, "I feel valued when my manager listens to my suggestions," you might code this as "managerial support."
3. **Search for Themes**: Group similar codes into overarching themes. For instance, codes like "managerial support" and "feedback acknowledgment" might fall under the theme "employee recognition."
4. **Review Themes**: Examine the themes for coherence and relevance, refining or combining them as necessary. Ensure that each theme captures a distinct aspect of the data.
5. **Define and Name Themes**: Clearly articulate what each theme represents and decide on concise, meaningful names. For example, "Barriers to Productivity" could be a theme summarizing codes like "interruptions" and "lack of resources."
6. **Produce a Report**: Use themes to build a coherent narrative, supported by representative quotes from participants, that addresses the research questions or objectives.

Advantages of Thematic Analysis

1. **Flexibility**: It can be applied to diverse datasets and research questions, accommodating a wide range of epistemological approaches.
2. **Accessibility**: Unlike advanced statistical methods, thematic analysis does not require specialized software or mathematical expertise, making it accessible to researchers at all levels.
3. **Depth and Richness**: By identifying underlying patterns, thematic analysis captures the richness of participants' experiences, providing nuanced insights.

Limitations of Thematic Analysis

1. **Subjectivity**: The researcher's interpretations heavily influence the results, which may introduce bias. Different researchers analyzing the same data could arrive at different themes.
2. **Time-Intensive**: Coding and reviewing large datasets can be labor-intensive and require meticulous attention to detail.
3. **Complexity of Large Datasets**: When applied to extensive qualitative datasets, the sheer volume of coding and theme refinement can become overwhelming without proper organization.
4. **Lack of Quantifiability**: Since thematic analysis focuses on patterns rather than frequencies, it is not suitable for studies requiring precise numerical representation.

By following a structured approach and remaining conscious of its limitations, thematic analysis allows researchers to unlock valuable insights from qualitative data and provide meaningful contributions to their field.

B.Content Analysis

Content analysis is a systematic technique used to quantify and analyze the presence, meanings, and relationships of specific words, phrases, or concepts within qualitative data. It is particularly effective when researchers aim to identify patterns, trends, or themes in textual or multimedia content. By breaking down data into manageable units and counting the frequency of occurrences, content analysis transforms qualitative information into quantitative insights. This method is invaluable for exploring large datasets, such as newspaper articles, company documents, social media posts, or policy reports, where manual interpretation would be impractical.

How Content Analysis Works

Content analysis begins by defining categories or codes that represent the key elements to be analyzed. These categories can be derived from the research objectives or the data itself. For instance, a study examining environmental discourse in corporate mission statements might define categories like "sustainability," "renewable energy," or "carbon footprint." Once the categories are established, researchers systematically code the text, marking occurrences of relevant words, phrases, or concepts.

After coding, researchers quantify the frequency of each category. For example, if "sustainability" appears 15 times in a set of mission statements, it signals its importance to the organizations studied. Advanced versions of content analysis go beyond simple word counts by analyzing the context in which terms appear or examining relationships between categories. This contextual understanding allows researchers to identify deeper meanings, such as whether "sustainability" is discussed as a value or merely as a marketing strategy.

Practical Example

Imagine a researcher studying how the media portrays artificial intelligence (AI). They analyze 500 newspaper articles, coding occurrences of words like "opportunity," "risk," "ethics," and "automation." Results might reveal that "risk" appears significantly more frequently than "opportunity," suggesting that the media frames AI more negatively than positively. This analysis could further identify patterns, such as which industries are most associated with these terms (e.g., "automation" in manufacturing).

Such insights are crucial for understanding public sentiment, shaping policies, or informing organizations on how to manage their messaging.

When to Use Content Analysis

1. **Quantifying Patterns in Large Text Datasets**: It is ideal for analyzing voluminous text-based content, such as thousands of social media posts, policy documents, or customer reviews, where manual analysis is unfeasible.
2. **Comparative Studies**: Useful for comparing the use of specific terms or ideas across different groups, such as organizations, media outlets, or geographic regions.
3. **Longitudinal Analysis**: Effective for examining how the use of certain terms or themes evolves over time. For example, researchers could track how the concept of "sustainability" has grown in corporate reporting over the past decade.
4. **Media or Communication Studies**: Commonly employed in journalism and media research to examine how specific topics are represented or framed in the public sphere.

Steps to Apply Content Analysis

1. **Define the Research Objectives**
   Clearly outline what you aim to achieve. For instance, are you trying to measure how often a company discusses innovation, or are you exploring broader societal themes in public speeches?
2. **Establish Categories or Codes**
   Decide on the categories of analysis. These can be predefined based on theory or emerge from the data itself (inductive coding). For example, analyzing product reviews might involve categories like "price," "quality," "delivery," and "customer service."
3. **Collect the Data**
   Gather textual or multimedia content relevant to your study. Sources can range from policy documents and newspapers to social media posts or advertisements. Ensure the dataset is comprehensive and representative.
4. **Code the Data**
   Break the content into units (e.g., sentences, paragraphs, or individual words) and assign codes based on predefined categories. For instance, if analyzing social media posts about electric vehicles, a comment like "Electric cars are expensive" would be coded under "cost concerns."
5. **Quantify and Analyze**
   Count the frequency of each code or category. Advanced analyses may include identifying co-occurrences (e.g., how often "cost" and "environmental benefits" are mentioned together) or studying the context of the terms.
6. **Interpret the Results**
   Use the quantitative data to draw meaningful conclusions. For instance, if "sustainability" is mentioned frequently but always in marketing contexts, it may suggest organizations are greenwashing rather than committing to sustainable practices.

Advantages of Content Analysis

1. **Versatility**: It can be applied to a wide range of materials, including written documents, speeches, multimedia content, and social media data.
2. **Quantitative and Qualitative Insights**: While primarily quantitative, content analysis also offers qualitative insights by examining the context and connotations of words or phrases.
3. **Systematic and Objective**: Its structured approach ensures consistency and reproducibility, especially when coding frameworks are well-defined.
4. **Longitudinal Capabilities**: It is effective for tracking changes over time, such as shifts in public discourse or corporate messaging.

Limitations of Content Analysis

1. **Loss of Context and Nuance**: Quantifying words or phrases may overlook their contextual meanings. For instance, "risk" might refer to different ideas in financial documents versus environmental reports.
2. **Subjectivity in Coding**: While systematic, content analysis still relies on researchers' judgment to define categories and interpret findings, which may introduce bias.
3. **Overemphasis on Frequency**: High word frequency does not necessarily equate to importance. A term appearing less frequently might carry greater significance in its context.
4. **Time-Consuming for Large Datasets**: While software tools like NVivo or Atlas.ti can assist, the initial coding and validation stages remain labor-intensive, especially for large datasets.
5. **Requires Theoretical Grounding**: Effective content analysis depends on a clear theoretical framework to guide the selection of categories and interpretation of results. Without it, findings may lack depth or relevance.

Advanced Applications

Modern tools like natural language processing (NLP) have expanded the potential of content analysis. Sentiment analysis, for example, evaluates the tone of text (e.g., positive, negative, neutral) in customer reviews or social media posts. Similarly, topic modeling algorithms automatically identify themes in large datasets, reducing reliance on manual coding.

By providing a systematic and quantifiable approach to analyzing qualitative data, content analysis bridges the gap between exploratory and confirmatory research, making it an indispensable tool for understanding textual patterns and trends.

C. *Narrative Analysis*

Narrative analysis is a qualitative research method that examines personal stories, accounts, or lived experiences to interpret human behavior, culture, or historical events. Unlike other methods that focus on coding and identifying broad patterns, narrative analysis explores how individuals construct and communicate meaning through their stories. By delving into narratives, researchers can uncover the complexities of human experiences, such as motivations, emotions, values, and social interactions. This method is particularly valuable for studying subjects where context, chronology, or personal interpretation plays a central role, such as life histories, career trajectories, or cultural shifts.

How Narrative Analysis Works

Narrative analysis begins with the collection of detailed stories, usually through interviews, autobiographies, oral histories, or archival records. The researcher pays close attention to how the story is told, including its structure, language, and sequence of events. For instance, a rural entrepreneur might narrate their journey of starting a business by describing key milestones, such as securing funding, navigating local markets, or overcoming social barriers.

The researcher then analyzes the narrative for patterns, themes, or key transitions. Unlike thematic analysis, which focuses on recurring ideas across a dataset, narrative analysis prioritizes the chronological order and coherence of an individual's story. It seeks to understand how people make sense of their experiences within specific social, cultural, or historical contexts. For example, a narrative might reveal that an entrepreneur's challenges are shaped not only by financial constraints but also by cultural expectations around gender roles.

Practical Example

Consider a study exploring the career paths of women leaders in traditionally male-dominated industries like construction or technology. Through narrative analysis, researchers could collect life stories of female leaders, focusing on their educational backgrounds, first job experiences, barriers faced (e.g., workplace bias), and eventual success strategies. The analysis might reveal common turning points, such as receiving mentorship or breaking stereotypes, and how these events influenced their leadership journeys. This detailed understanding provides depth and richness that statistical data alone cannot capture.

When to Use Narrative Analysis

1. **Exploring Personal Experiences**

   Narrative analysis is most effective when the research question revolves around individual experiences or subjective realities. For example, studying the mental health challenges faced by frontline healthcare workers during the COVID-19 pandemic could benefit from narrative analysis to understand the emotional toll and coping mechanisms.

2. **Studying Historical or Cultural Events**

   It is highly suitable for examining events within specific historical or cultural contexts. For instance, analyzing oral histories from freedom fighters in India's independence movement could shed light on their motivations and collective struggles.

3. **Examining Social Constructs**

   Narratives often reflect broader societal influences, such as gender norms, class dynamics, or cultural traditions. For example, life stories of women in rural areas pursuing education can reveal how societal barriers and support systems interact to shape their opportunities.

4. **Understanding Transitions or Turning Points**

   When the focus is on major life changes or transitions (e.g., migration, career shifts, or personal loss), narrative analysis helps identify the significance of these events in the broader context of the individual's life.

Steps to Apply Narrative Analysis

1. **Collect Narratives**

   Gather stories through in-depth interviews, oral histories, diaries, or autobiographies. Ensure that the participants are encouraged to share their experiences in their own words, without interruption or leading questions.

2. **Transcribe and Organize Data**

   Convert oral stories into written transcripts, preserving the flow and language of the narrative. Structure the stories chronologically or by major themes for ease of analysis.

3. **Analyze the Structure of the Narrative**

   Examine how the story is constructed. Identify the beginning (introduction of events or challenges), middle (actions taken, transitions), and end (resolution or outcomes). For instance, a migrant worker's story might begin with economic struggles, describe the decision to move cities, and end with newfound stability or further challenges.

4. **Identify Key Events and Themes**

   Highlight critical events, transitions, or recurring ideas that provide insights into the individual's experiences. Focus on how the participant interprets these events, rather than imposing external judgments.

5. **Contextualize the Narrative**

   Place the story within its broader social, cultural, or historical context. For example, an entrepreneur's account of starting a business in a rural area must be analyzed in light of local infrastructure, market accessibility, and cultural norms.

6. **Interpret the Findings**

   Use the analysis to build a rich, contextualized understanding of the participant's experiences. Present the findings as case studies, descriptive accounts, or thematic summaries.

Advantages of Narrative Analysis

1. **Captures Depth and Complexity**

   Narrative analysis uncovers the richness of individual experiences, providing nuanced insights that go beyond numbers or predefined categories. It highlights subjective realities and emotional depth.

2. **Preserves Chronological Flow**

   Unlike other qualitative methods, it emphasizes the sequence of events, allowing researchers to understand how experiences unfold over time. This is particularly useful for studying life trajectories or historical developments.

3. **Explores Social and Cultural Contexts**
Narratives often reflect societal and cultural influences, offering insights into how broader forces shape individual lives. For example, examining stories of refugees can reveal the interplay between displacement, identity, and resilience.

4. **Flexible and Inclusive**
This method can be adapted for diverse research topics and participant groups, from personal interviews to archival data. It is particularly inclusive for marginalized voices often overlooked in traditional research.

Limitations of Narrative Analysis

1. **Subjectivity and Bias**
Narrative analysis relies heavily on the researcher's interpretation of the data, which can introduce bias. For instance, different researchers analyzing the same story might emphasize different aspects based on their perspectives.

2. **Limited Generalizability**
Since narrative analysis focuses on individual stories, the findings may not apply broadly across populations. For example, analyzing the life story of one rural entrepreneur might not reflect the challenges faced by others in different regions or industries.

3. **Time-Intensive**
Collecting, transcribing, and analyzing narratives is a labor-intensive process, requiring significant effort to ensure accuracy and depth.

4. **Dependence on Participant Recall**
Narratives often rely on participants' memories, which may be incomplete or biased. For example, a participant may unintentionally omit key details or overemphasize certain events based on their current perspective.

5. **Complexity of Analysis**
Unlike methods with clear-cut coding or statistical outputs, narrative analysis requires interpretive skills to weave data into meaningful insights. Beginners may find it challenging to handle the richness of qualitative narratives effectively.

Advanced Applications of Narrative Analysis

1. **Policy Development**
Narrative analysis can help policymakers understand the lived experiences of target populations, ensuring that policies address real needs. For instance, analyzing farmers' accounts of climate change impacts can guide agricultural policies.

2. **Healthcare Research**
In medical and psychological studies, narrative analysis is often used to understand patients' journeys through illness, treatment, and recovery. It provides insights into their emotional and social experiences, complementing clinical data.

3. **Education and Learning**
Teachers and education researchers can use narrative analysis to examine students' learning experiences, uncovering barriers to engagement or factors contributing to success.

By emphasizing personal stories and their broader contexts, narrative analysis provides a unique lens for understanding human experiences. While it requires careful interpretation, its depth and richness make it an indispensable tool in qualitative research.

2. Quantitative Data Analysis

Quantitative analysis applies mathematical or statistical methods to analyze numeric data, such as survey scores or experimental measurements. It is used for hypothesis testing, measuring relationships, and drawing generalizable conclusions.

Descriptive Statistics
Descriptive statistics summarize datasets to highlight their central tendencies, variability, and distribution.

A. Mean (Average)

The **mean**, also known as the arithmetic average, is one of the most commonly used measures of central tendency in statistics. It represents the central value of a dataset and provides an overall summary by considering all the data points. The mean is calculated by summing all the values in the dataset and dividing the total by the number of observations. For example, if you want to calculate the average age of employees in a company, you would add up the ages of all employees and divide that sum by the total number of employees.

The mean is widely used in both academic research and practical applications because it captures the "center" of the data in a straightforward manner. However, its effectiveness depends on the nature of the dataset and the presence (or absence) of extreme values, which can significantly distort the result.

How to Calculate the Mean
To calculate the mean, follow these steps:

1. Add all the data points in the dataset. This is called the **sum of the observations**.
2. Count the total number of data points. This is referred to as the **number of observations** (denoted as n).
3. Divide the sum of the data points by the number of observations.

Mathematically, the formula for the mean is:

$$\text{Mean} = \frac{\text{Sum of all data points}}{\text{Number of observations}}$$

Example: Suppose a company has five employees with ages 25, 30, 35, 40, and 45. The mean age is calculated as:

$$\text{Mean} = \frac{25 + 30 + 35 + 40 + 45}{5} = \frac{175}{5} = 35$$

This means the average age of employees is 35 years.

When to Use the Mean

1. **For Symmetrically Distributed Data**
   The mean is most appropriate when the data is symmetrically distributed (i.e., it follows a normal distribution or bell curve) and there are no extreme values (outliers). In such cases, the mean accurately represents the center of the dataset.
   Example: If test scores in a classroom range from 50 to 100 and are evenly distributed, the mean test score provides a reliable summary of overall student performance.

2. **For Continuous Data**
   The mean works well for continuous variables, such as height, weight, income, or temperature, where values can take any point within a range.
3. **When Comparing Groups**
   The mean is useful for comparing the central tendency of different groups. For example, comparing the mean sales revenue of two companies can help determine which performs better on average.
4. **For Data with Equal Weighting**
   Use the mean when each observation in the dataset carries equal importance or weight. If some observations are more significant than others, a weighted mean may be more appropriate.

When NOT to Use the Mean

1. **In Skewed Datasets**
   When the dataset is skewed, meaning it contains extreme values (outliers), the mean can be misleading. For example, in a dataset of incomes, a few extremely high salaries might inflate the mean, making it unrepresentative of the typical income. In such cases, the **median** is a better measure of central tendency.

   Example: If the incomes in a dataset are ₹20,000, ₹25,000, ₹30,000, ₹35,000, and ₹1,00,000, the mean would be:

   $$\text{Mean} = \frac{20,000 + 25,000 + 30,000 + 35,000 + 1,00,000}{5} = \frac{2,10,000}{5} = ₹42,000$$

   However, the median income (₹30,000) is a better representation because the extreme value of ₹1,00,000 distorts the mean.

2. **For Categorical Data**
   The mean is not applicable for categorical variables like gender, job title, or customer satisfaction levels. For such data, the **mode** (most frequent value) is more appropriate.
3. **For Data with Unequal Importance**
   When certain observations carry more weight than others, the mean is not ideal unless adjusted using a weighted formula.
4. **For Open-Ended Data**
   If the dataset contains open-ended values (e.g., "above ₹1,00,000"), the mean cannot be calculated accurately without exact numbers.

Advantages of the Mean

1. **Simple to Calculate and Understand**
   The mean is easy to compute and provides a quick snapshot of the dataset's central value, making it accessible for researchers and practitioners.
2. **Uses All Data Points**
   Unlike the mode or median, the mean considers all values in the dataset, providing a comprehensive summary of the data.
3. **Basis for Advanced Statistical Methods**
   The mean is foundational in advanced statistical techniques, such as standard deviation, variance, and hypothesis

testing. It serves as a reference point for understanding data distribution.

4. **Useful for Normally Distributed Data**
When the dataset follows a normal distribution, the mean is an excellent representation of the center, as it aligns closely with the median and mode.

Limitations of the Mean

1. **Sensitive to Outliers**
Extreme values can distort the mean, making it an unreliable measure of central tendency for skewed datasets. For example, one extremely high or low value in a dataset can pull the mean away from the majority of data points.
2. **Misleading for Skewed Distributions**
In datasets with a long tail (e.g., income or housing prices), the mean may overestimate or underestimate the typical value, leading to incorrect conclusions.
3. **Cannot Be Used for Ordinal or Nominal Data**
The mean is unsuitable for data where values are ranked (ordinal) or labeled (nominal). For example, calculating the mean of satisfaction levels on a scale of "Very Satisfied," "Neutral," and "Very Dissatisfied" is meaningless.
4. **Lacks Contextual Understanding**
The mean alone provides no information about data variability or how individual data points differ from the average. For example, knowing that the average test score is 75% does not reveal whether most students scored close to this value or if there was significant variation.

Practical Applications of the Mean

1. **Business and Finance**

   - Businesses use the mean to calculate average sales, revenue, or profit margins. For example, determining the average sales per store helps assess overall performance.
   - Financial analysts calculate the mean return on investment (ROI) to evaluate investment performance.

2. **Healthcare**

   - The mean is used to calculate average patient recovery times, medication dosages, or hospital occupancy rates. For instance, determining the average time for post-surgery recovery aids resource planning.

3. **Education**

   - Educators use the mean to summarize student test scores, helping identify areas for curriculum improvement. For example, if the mean score for a mathematics test is low, it may indicate gaps in teaching methods.

4. **Public Policy**

   - Policymakers calculate mean income, literacy rates, or unemployment rates to assess socio-economic conditions and design targeted interventions.

5. **Sports Analytics**

   - The mean is frequently used to calculate average performance metrics, such as the mean number of goals scored per game or the mean batting average of a cricket player.

By understanding the strengths and limitations of the mean, researchers and practitioners can decide when it is the most appropriate measure of central tendency and when alternative methods, like the median or mode, would be more suitable.

Median

The **median** is a statistical measure of central tendency that represents the middle value in an ordered dataset. Unlike the mean, which sums all values and divides by the number of observations, the median identifies the point where half the data lies below it and half lies above it. In datasets with an odd number of values, the median is the exact middle value. For datasets with an even number of values, the median is calculated as the average of the two middle values. The median is particularly useful when the dataset contains outliers or is not symmetrically distributed, as it is not affected by extreme values.

For instance, if we want to calculate the median household income in a community, we first arrange all income values in ascending order and then find the middle value. If the incomes are ₹20,000, ₹25,000, ₹30,000, ₹35,000, and ₹10,00,000, the median is ₹30,000, which provides a better representation of typical household income than the mean (₹2,32,000), which is skewed by the extreme value of ₹10,00,000.

How to Calculate the Median

1. **Organize the Data in Ascending Order**
   Start by arranging all data points from the smallest to the largest. This step ensures that the values are ordered correctly for identifying the central value.
2. **Identify the Middle Point**

   - For datasets with an odd number of values, the median is the middle value.
     Example: If the dataset is 15, 20, 25, 30, 35, the median is 25 (the third value in the ordered list).

For datasets with an even number of values, calculate the average of the two middle values.

Example: If the dataset is 15, 20, 25, 30, the median is:

$$\text{Median} = \frac{20 + 25}{2} = 22.5$$

3. **Verify for Outliers or Skewness**
   Check whether the dataset contains extreme values, as this will help determine whether the median is a better choice than the mean for representing central tendency.

When to Use the Median

1. **For Skewed Data**
   The median is ideal for datasets with a skewed distribution, where extreme values (outliers) can distort the mean. For instance, in a dataset of employee salaries where most earn between ₹20,000 and ₹50,000 but a few executives earn over ₹5,00,000, the median provides a more accurate reflection of the typical salary.

2. **For Ordinal Data**

When the data is ordinal (ranked categories), the median is the best measure of central tendency because it identifies the midpoint without requiring precise numerical intervals. For example, satisfaction ratings (e.g., "very dissatisfied" to "very satisfied") can use the median to determine the central tendency.

3. **When Outliers are Present**

The median is robust to outliers, making it suitable for datasets with extreme values. For instance, analyzing housing prices in a city where a few luxury mansions skew the data can benefit from using the median instead of the mean.

4. **For Small Datasets**

In small datasets, the median remains a simple and reliable measure of central tendency, especially when there is variability in the data.

Advantages of the Median

1. **Not Affected by Outliers**

Unlike the mean, the median is unaffected by extreme values. This makes it a better representation of central tendency for datasets where outliers significantly distort the mean.

Example: In a dataset of home prices (₹10 lakh, ₹20 lakh, ₹30 lakh, ₹40 lakh, ₹10 crore), the mean home price is ₹2.6 crore, which is misleading. The median, ₹30 lakh, more accurately reflects the central value.

2. **Works Well for Skewed Distributions**

When data is not symmetrically distributed, such as income levels, the median is more representative of the central tendency than the mean.

3. **Simple to Compute**

Calculating the median involves basic ordering and identifying the middle value, making it easy to use, even for beginners.

4. **Applicable to Ordinal Data**

The median can be used with ordinal data, such as survey responses or rankings, where numerical calculations like the mean are inappropriate.

5. **Resistant to Misleading Interpretations**

Since the median focuses only on the middle value, it avoids being skewed by the variability of extreme values at either end of the dataset.

Disadvantages of the Median

1. **Does Not Consider All Data Points**

Unlike the mean, which takes all values into account, the median focuses only on the middle value, potentially losing information about the dataset as a whole.

2. **Not Suitable for Symmetrical Data**

For symmetrically distributed datasets without outliers, the mean provides a more comprehensive summary than the median, as it incorporates every data point.

3. **Limited in Advanced Analysis**

The median is rarely used in advanced statistical calculations, such as variance or regression, where the mean is a standard measure.

4. **Challenges with Categorical Data**

The median cannot be calculated for nominal data, such as gender or eye color, as these lack an inherent order or ranking.

5. **Less Sensitive to Data Changes**

Small changes to values in the dataset may not affect the median, potentially reducing its sensitivity in reflecting data trends.

Practical Applications of the Median

1. **Income and Wealth Analysis**
   Economists and policymakers frequently use the median to analyze income distribution. For instance, the median household income is often reported instead of the mean to avoid distortions caused by extremely high-income earners.
2. **Real Estate**
   The median house price is commonly used to represent the central value of property markets, as it is less affected by a few extremely high or low prices.
3. **Healthcare**
   In analyzing patient recovery times, the median can provide a reliable summary, especially if a few patients experience unusually long or short recovery periods due to complications.
4. **Education**
   Median test scores are used to measure typical student performance in a class, particularly when the dataset contains outliers, such as students with exceptionally high or low scores.
5. **Sports Analytics**
   The median is used to represent player salaries, as the presence of superstar athletes earning disproportionately high salaries can inflate the mean and misrepresent the financial dynamics of a team.

Real-World Example: Median vs. Mean
Imagine you are analyzing the monthly incomes of a group of 10 employees in an organization:

$$₹25,000, ₹28,000, ₹30,000, ₹35,000, ₹40,000, ₹45,000, ₹50,000, ₹55,000, ₹60,000, ₹5,00,000$$

- **Mean:**

$$\text{Mean} = \frac{25,000 + 28,000 + \cdots + 5,00,000}{10} = ₹89,800$$

The mean is distorted by the single outlier (₹5,00,000), giving an unrealistic picture of the typical income.

- **Median:**

After ordering the data, the median is calculated as the average of the two middle values:

$$\text{Median} = \frac{40,000 + 45,000}{2} = ₹42,500$$

The median provides much more accurate representation of the central income.

By focusing on the middle value, the median is an essential tool in data analysis, especially for skewed datasets or when outliers are present. Its simplicity, robustness, and practical applications make it a valuable measure of central tendency across diverse fields.

C. Mode

The **mode** is a measure of central tendency that represents the value appearing most frequently in a dataset. Unlike the mean or median, which involve mathematical calculations, the mode is determined simply by identifying the most common data point(s). It is particularly useful for datasets where certain values occur repeatedly and provides insight into what is "most typical" or "most popular" within the data.

For instance, if a store tracks the sizes of shirts sold in a week and the dataset is:
M, M, M, L, L, XL, XL, XL, S, M, the **mode** is **M (Medium)** because it occurs most frequently (four times). This indicates that "Medium" is the most popular size among customers, which could guide inventory decisions.

How to Identify the Mode

1. **List the Dataset**: Organize the data and note how often each value appears. For example, in the dataset {4, 4, 5, 6, 6, 6, 7}, the frequency of each value is:

   - 4: Appears twice.
   - 5: Appears once.
   - 6: Appears three times.
   - 7: Appears once.

2. **Determine the Frequency**: Identify the value with the highest frequency. In the example above, the mode is **6** because it appears three times, more often than any other value.

3. **Handle Multimodal or No-Mode Cases**:

   - If two or more values occur with the same highest frequency, the dataset is **multimodal**. For instance, in {3, 3, 5, 5, 7, 8}, the modes are **3 and 5**.
   - If no value repeats, the dataset is said to have **no mode**.

When to Use the Mode

1. **For Nominal or Categorical Data**
   The mode is the only measure of central tendency applicable to nominal data, such as gender, product categories, or customer preferences. For instance, if a survey reveals that "Instagram" is the most frequently mentioned favorite social media platform, the mode reflects the most popular choice.

2. **For Identifying Popularity**
   The mode helps identify the most common value in a dataset, such as the most frequently purchased product or the most common test score in a classroom.

3. **For Multimodal Data**
   When there are multiple peaks in data distribution, the mode highlights these distinct clusters, providing insights into patterns. For instance, a dataset of clothing sales might have modes for "Medium" and "Large," indicating demand for multiple sizes.

4. **When Simplicity is Needed**
   The mode is straightforward to calculate and interpret, making it useful for quick assessments or when working with small datasets.

Advantages of the Mode

1. **Ease of Calculation**
   The mode requires no mathematical computations, making it simple to determine, even for non-technical users.

2. **Works for Categorical Data**
   The mode is the only measure of central tendency that applies to non-numeric data, such as preferences or

categories.

3. **Highlights Typical Values**

   By identifying the most frequent value, the mode provides insights into what is most common or preferred within a dataset.

4. **Handles Multimodal Distributions**

   In datasets with multiple peaks, the mode identifies all prominent clusters, offering a richer understanding of the data.

Limitations of the Mode

1. **Lack of Uniqueness**

   A dataset can have no mode or multiple modes, which reduces its reliability as a single summary measure. For example, in {2, 2, 3, 3, 4}, both 2 and 3 are modes, making it less clear which is more representative.

2. **Not Suitable for Continuous Data**

   The mode is rarely used for continuous numerical data, where values do not repeat often, such as temperatures or weights.

3. **Ignores Entire Dataset**

   The mode focuses only on the most frequent value(s), ignoring other data points, which might result in loss of information. For example, if one test score occurs frequently while others vary widely, the mode doesn't reflect the overall distribution.

4. **Not Useful for Advanced Analysis**

   Unlike the mean, the mode cannot be used in advanced statistical calculations, such as regression or variance analysis.

Practical Applications of the Mode

1. **Business and Marketing**

   - Companies use the mode to determine the most popular product, color, or size, helping them optimize inventory and production.
   - For example, a car manufacturer might identify the most requested color (e.g., "White") and prioritize its production.

2. **Education**

   - In classrooms, the mode can identify the most common grade or score, highlighting patterns in student performance.

3. **Healthcare**

   - Hospitals use the mode to track the most frequently occurring diagnoses or treatments, aiding resource planning.

4. **Public Policy**

   - Governments use the mode to identify the most common demographic characteristics in surveys (e.g., household size) when designing policies.

5. **Customer Feedback**

   - Companies analyze customer feedback to find the most frequently mentioned issue or request, ensuring they address the most pressing concerns.

Inferential Statistics

While the mode is a descriptive statistic, **inferential statistics** go a step further, allowing researchers to make generalizations about a population based on sample data.

Definition and Purpose

Inferential statistics use data from a sample to infer conclusions about the larger population. This process involves estimating population parameters, testing hypotheses, and making predictions. For example, a company surveying 500 customers about their satisfaction can use inferential techniques to predict satisfaction levels among their entire customer base.

Key Components of Inferential Statistics

1. **Population and Sample**

   - **Population**: The entire group you are interested in studying (e.g., all employees in a company).
   - **Sample**: A smaller subset of the population used to draw conclusions (e.g., 200 randomly selected employees).

2. **Hypothesis Testing**

   - Researchers use inferential statistics to test hypotheses and determine whether observed results are statistically significant. For example, testing whether a new teaching method improves student scores compared to the old method.

3. **Confidence Intervals**

   - These provide a range of values within which the true population parameter is likely to fall. For instance, if a survey estimates that 60% of customers are satisfied, a confidence interval might specify the satisfaction rate is between 57% and 63%.

4. **Generalization**

   - Inferential techniques allow researchers to apply findings from a sample to the entire population, provided the sample is representative.

How Inferential Statistics Relate to the Mode

While the mode summarizes the most frequent observation in a dataset, inferential statistics help determine whether the observed pattern (e.g., most customers preferring a product) applies consistently across the entire population. For example, if "Medium" is the most sold shirt size in a sample of 1,000 sales, inferential methods can estimate whether this pattern holds for all future sales.

By integrating descriptive tools like the mode with inferential techniques, researchers can both summarize existing data and make informed predictions.

Inferential Statistics

Inferential statistics is a branch of statistics that enables researchers to draw conclusions, make predictions, and test hypotheses about a population using data from a smaller, representative sample. Unlike descriptive statistics, which summarizes and organizes data, inferential statistics focuses on understanding the larger context by analyzing patterns, relationships, and differences within the data.

For instance, a researcher cannot survey every customer of a global company, but by analyzing a sample of customer responses, inferential statistics can estimate satisfaction levels for the entire customer base. Similarly, inferential statistics help in testing whether observed results (e.g., the effectiveness of a new teaching method) are due to chance or reflect true differences.

Key Concepts in Inferential Statistics

1. **Population vs. Sample**

   - **Population**: The complete group of interest (e.g., all college students in India).
   - **Sample**: A subset of the population chosen for analysis (e.g., 500 randomly selected students).

2. **Hypothesis Testing**

   - Inferential statistics involves testing hypotheses to determine whether observed patterns are statistically significant.

3. **Statistical Significance**

   - This determines whether results are likely due to a real effect rather than random chance. A p-value (usually ≤ 0.05) is used to assess significance.

4. **Confidence Intervals**

   - Inferential methods estimate a range within which the true population parameter is likely to fall, with a given level of confidence (e.g., 95%).

5. **Statistical Tests**

   - Common inferential tests include t-tests, chi-square tests, ANOVA, and regression, each designed to analyze specific research questions or data types.

T-Test

A **t-test** is one of the most widely used inferential statistical tests for comparing the means of two groups to determine whether the observed differences are statistically significant. Developed by William Sealy Gosset under the pseudonym "Student," the t-test is ideal for assessing whether differences in group means reflect real effects or are likely due to random variation.

How the T-Test Works

The t-test evaluates whether the difference between the means of two groups is large enough to be unlikely due to chance. It considers the variability of the data and the sample size to calculate a t-statistic, which is then compared against a critical value from a t-distribution table.

1. **Formulate Hypotheses:**

   - **Null Hypothesis (H⁰):** There is no significant difference between the group means.
   - **Alternative Hypothesis (H₁):** There is a significant difference between the group means.

2. **Calculate the T-Statistic:**
   The t-statistic is calculated based on the difference between the group means, divided by the standard error of the difference.

$$t = \frac{\bar{X}_1 - \bar{X}_2}{\sqrt{\dfrac{s_1^2}{n_1} + \dfrac{s_2^2}{n_2}}}$$

Where:

- $\bar{X}_1, \bar{X}_2$: Means of the two groups.

- s_1^2, s_2^2: Variances of the two groups.

- n_1, n_2: Sample sizes of the two groups.

Compare to the Critical Value:

Compare the calculated t-statistic to the critical value from the t-distribution table (based on degrees of freedom and significance level). If the t-statistic exceeds the critical value, the null hypothesis is rejected.

3. **Assess Statistical Significance:**
   Alternatively, a p-value can be used to determine significance. If the p-value ≤ 0.05, the result is considered statistically significant.

Types of T-Tests

1. **Independent Samples T-Test:**
   Compares the means of two independent groups, such as male vs. female or experimental group vs. control group.
   Example: Testing whether a new teaching method improves student performance compared to a traditional method by comparing the average test scores of two separate groups.
2. **Paired Samples T-Test:**
   Compares means within the same group at two different points in time or under two different conditions.
   Example: Measuring the effectiveness of a training program by comparing employees' test scores before and after the training.
3. **One-Sample T-Test:**
   Compares the mean of a single group to a known value or benchmark.
   Example: Testing whether the average blood pressure in a community differs from the national average.

When to Use a T-Test

1. **Comparing Two Groups:**
   The t-test is ideal when the research involves assessing differences between two groups, such as treatment vs.

control or male vs. female.

2. **Continuous Data**:
Use a t-test when the dependent variable is continuous (e.g., test scores, income, height).

3. **Normally Distributed Data**:
The t-test assumes that the data follows a normal distribution. For non-normal data, non-parametric alternatives like the Mann-Whitney U test should be used.

4. **Small Sample Sizes**:
The t-test is specifically designed for smaller sample sizes (typically n<30), although it remains applicable for larger samples.

Limitations of the T-Test

1. **Assumes Normal Distribution**:
The t-test relies on the assumption that the data is normally distributed. For datasets that do not meet this criterion, results may be inaccurate.

2. **Sensitive to Outliers**:
Extreme values can skew the results, leading to incorrect conclusions. Outlier removal or robust methods are necessary for reliable analysis.

3. **Limited to Two Groups**:
The t-test can only compare two groups. For comparisons involving three or more groups, methods like ANOVA should be used.

4. **Sample Size Dependence**:
The accuracy of the t-test decreases with very small sample sizes (n<10) because variability becomes more pronounced.

Practical Example of a T-Test

Research Question: Does a new teaching method improve student performance compared to a traditional method?

- **Step 1**: Divide students into two groups: one using the new teaching method and the other using the traditional method.
- **Step 2**: Administer the same test to both groups and record their scores.
- **Step 3**: Calculate the mean score for each group (e.g., new method = 85, traditional method = 78).
- **Step 4**: Use an independent samples t-test to evaluate whether the difference (85 vs. 78) is statistically significant.

Interpretation: If the p-value is less than 0.05, the difference is significant, suggesting the new teaching method is more effective.

Advantages of the T-Test

1. **Simplicity**:
The t-test is straightforward to perform and interpret, making it accessible to researchers with basic statistical knowledge.

2. **Versatility**:
It can be applied to diverse fields, including education, healthcare, business, and psychology, for evaluating group differences.

3. **Robustness with Small Samples**:
The t-test is effective for analyzing small sample sizes, where other methods may lack precision.

4. **Foundation for Advanced Analysis**:
   The t-test forms the basis for more complex techniques like ANOVA and regression, making it a foundational tool in statistics.

The t-test is a powerful and versatile statistical tool for comparing group means and testing hypotheses. By ensuring its assumptions are met and understanding its limitations, researchers can confidently use the t-test to make meaningful inferences about populations based on sample data. Whether evaluating new interventions, comparing treatments, or assessing group differences, the t-test remains an essential method in inferential statistics.

Regression Analysis

Regression analysis is a statistical method used to examine the relationship between one dependent variable (outcome) and one or more independent variables (predictors). By quantifying this relationship, regression helps researchers determine the strength, direction, and nature of the connection between variables. It also allows for predictions and explanations of how changes in independent variables influence the dependent variable.

For example, a company might use regression analysis to test whether advertising spend predicts sales revenue. If the analysis reveals a strong positive relationship, it indicates that increasing the advertising budget is likely to lead to higher sales. This information can guide resource allocation decisions.

Regression is widely used in various fields, including business, economics, healthcare, and social sciences, to analyze cause-and-effect relationships and make informed decisions.

How Regression Analysis Works

1. **Identify Variables**:

   - **Dependent Variable (Y)**: The outcome you want to predict or explain. For instance, "sales revenue."
   - **Independent Variables (X)**: The predictors or factors influencing the dependent variable. For example, "advertising spend" or "number of sales calls."

2. **Formulate the Regression Equation**:
   The relationship between variables is expressed using the regression equation:

$$Y = \beta_0 + \beta_1 X + \epsilon$$

   Where:

   - Y: Dependent variable.

   - β_0: Intercept (the value of Y when $X = 0$).

   - β_1: Slope (indicating how much Y changes for a one-unit change in X).

   - X: Independent variable.

   - ϵ: Error term (captures unexplained variance).

3. **Estimate Coefficients**:
   Statistical software calculates the coefficients (β_0 and β_1) that minimize the difference between observed and

predicted values of Y (using the least squares method).

4. **Assess Fit and Significance:**

   - The **R-squared value** indicates the proportion of variation in the dependent variable explained by the independent variable(s).
   - The **p-value** tests the statistical significance of coefficients.

5. **Interpret Results:**
   The coefficients and statistical outputs are used to explain the relationship and predict outcomes.

Types of Regression Analysis

1. **Simple Linear Regression**
   Examines the relationship between one independent variable and one dependent variable.
   Example: Predicting sales revenue (Y) based on advertising spend (X).
2. **Multiple Linear Regression**
   Involves two or more independent variables predicting a single dependent variable.
   Example: Analyzing how advertising spend (X1) and sales staff size (X2) jointly influence sales revenue (Y).
3. **Logistic Regression**
   Used when the dependent variable is binary or categorical (e.g., "yes/no" or "success/failure").
   Example: Predicting whether a customer will buy a product (1) or not (0) based on marketing efforts.
4. **Polynomial Regression**
   Models non-linear relationships by including polynomial terms of independent variables.
   Example: Analyzing the effect of age (X) on income (Y), where the relationship is not strictly linear.
5. **Ridge, Lasso, and Elastic Net Regression**
   Advanced regression techniques used to handle multicollinearity or high-dimensional data.

When to Use Regression Analysis

1. **For Cause-and-Effect Relationships**
   Regression is ideal for exploring how changes in independent variables affect the dependent variable. For instance, testing whether education level predicts job performance.
2. **To Predict Outcomes**
   Regression is used to forecast future values of the dependent variable based on known values of independent variables. For example, predicting sales for the next quarter based on historical advertising data.
3. **When Analyzing Continuous Data**
   Regression is most effective when variables are continuous, such as income, age, or temperature.
4. **To Control for Confounding Variables**
   Multiple regression helps control for additional variables that may influence the outcome, providing a clearer understanding of the relationship between key variables.

Advantages of Regression Analysis

1. **Quantifies Relationships**
   Regression not only identifies relationships but also quantifies their strength and direction. For example, it can show that for every ₹10,000 increase in advertising, sales revenue increases by ₹50,000.
2. **Predictive Power**
   Regression is a powerful tool for making predictions, helping businesses and policymakers anticipate outcomes

based on existing data.

3. **Flexibility**

Regression can handle multiple variables, complex relationships, and non-linear trends, making it suitable for diverse research problems.

4. **Control for Multiple Factors**

By including multiple independent variables, regression accounts for confounding factors, providing more accurate insights.

Limitations of Regression Analysis

1. **Sensitive to Multicollinearity**

Multicollinearity occurs when independent variables are highly correlated, making it difficult to isolate their individual effects. For instance, if both "number of employees" and "office size" are included as predictors, their overlap may distort results. Advanced techniques like ridge regression can mitigate this issue.

2. **Requires Linearity**

Standard regression assumes a linear relationship between variables. For non-linear patterns, alternative techniques like polynomial regression are required.

3. **Influenced by Outliers**

Extreme values can disproportionately affect regression coefficients, leading to biased results. Detecting and handling outliers (e.g., through robust regression) is critical.

4. **Overfitting**

Including too many variables in the model can lead to overfitting, where the regression captures random noise rather than meaningful patterns, reducing its predictive accuracy for new data.

5. **Assumes Normality and Homoscedasticity**

Regression assumes that residuals (errors) are normally distributed and have constant variance. Violations of these assumptions can lead to unreliable results.

Practical Example of Regression Analysis

Scenario: A retailer wants to understand how advertising spend influences monthly sales revenue.

1. **Variables**:

   - Dependent Variable (Y): Monthly sales revenue.
   - Independent Variable (X): Advertising spend.

2. **Regression Equation**:

After running the regression analysis, the equation is estimated as:

$Y = 50,000 + 5X$

This means that:

   - The baseline sales (when advertising spend is zero) are ₹50,000.
   - For every ₹1 increase in advertising spend, sales revenue increases by ₹5.

3. **Insights**:

If the company spends ₹10,000 on advertising, the predicted sales are:

$Y = 50,000 + 5(10,000) = ₹1,00,000$

4. **Decision:**
   Based on these results, the retailer can allocate budgets to optimize advertising spend and maximize sales.

Applications of Regression Analysis

1. **Business and Marketing**

   - Predicting sales revenue based on advertising spend or customer traffic.
   - Analyzing factors affecting customer satisfaction or product demand.

2. **Healthcare**

   - Studying how age, diet, and exercise affect blood pressure or disease risk.

3. **Social Sciences**

   - Examining how education and income influence life satisfaction or political preferences.

4. **Economics**

   - Analyzing the impact of inflation, unemployment, or government policies on economic growth.

5. **Environmental Studies**

   - Exploring how temperature and rainfall affect crop yields or ecosystem health.

Regression analysis is a cornerstone of inferential statistics, offering robust tools for understanding relationships, testing hypotheses, and making predictions. By carefully addressing its assumptions and limitations, researchers can harness its full potential to derive actionable insights.

Chi-Square Test

The **chi-square test** is a statistical method used to determine whether there is a significant association between two categorical variables. It evaluates whether the observed frequencies in a dataset differ from expected frequencies under the assumption of no relationship (null hypothesis). This test is particularly useful when working with nominal (e.g., gender, product categories) or ordinal data.

For example, a researcher might use a chi-square test to examine whether gender influences product preferences, such as whether men and women differ significantly in their choice of smartphones versus laptops. By comparing the actual purchase patterns to expected frequencies (if gender had no influence), the chi-square test determines if the relationship is statistically significant.

How the Chi-Square Test Works

1. **Hypotheses Formulation:**

   - **Null Hypothesis (H^0):** Assumes no relationship exists between the variables (e.g., gender does not influence product preference).
   - **Alternative Hypothesis (H_1):** Assumes a relationship exists (e.g., gender influences product preference).

2. **Construct a Contingency Table:**

Create a table showing the observed frequencies (actual counts) for each combination of categories. For example:

Gender	Smartphones	Laptops	Total
Male	50	30	80
Female	40	60	100
Total	90	90	180

3. **Calculate Expected Frequencies**:
    For each cell, calculate the expected frequency using:

$$\text{Expected Frequency} = \frac{\text{Row Total} \times \text{Column Total}}{\text{Grand Total}}$$

For instance, the expected frequency for males purchasing smartphones is:

$$\text{Expected Frequency} = \frac{80 \times 90}{180} = 40$$

4. Apply the Chi-Square Formula:

Use the chi-square formula to compare observed (O) and expected (E) frequencies:

$$\chi^2 = \sum \frac{(O - E)^2}{E}$$

For example, if $O = 50$ and $E = 40$ for males purchasing smartphones, the contribution to chi-square is:

$$\frac{(50 - 40)^2}{40} = \frac{10^2}{40} = 2.5$$

Repeat this calculation for all cells and sum the results to obtain the chi-square statistic (χ^2).

5. Compare to the Critical Value:

Compare the calculated χ^2 statistic to the critical value from the chi-square distribution table (based on degrees of freedom and significance level).

6. Interpret the Result:

If χ^2 exceeds the critical value or the p-value is less than the chosen significance level (e.g., 0.05), reject the null hypothesis. This indicates a significant relationship between the variables.

When to Use the Chi-Square Test

1. **For Categorical Data**
    The chi-square test is ideal for analyzing nominal or ordinal data, such as gender, voting preferences, or product

categories.

2. **Testing Relationships**

Use this test to determine whether two variables are associated. For example, examining if location influences voting patterns.

3. **Survey and Experimental Data**

The test is often applied to survey responses or experimental data to evaluate patterns in categorical outcomes (e.g., yes/no, agree/disagree).

4. **Adequate Sample Size**

The test requires a sufficiently large sample size to produce reliable results. Each expected frequency should ideally be at least 5.

Advantages of the Chi-Square Test

1. **Non-Parametric**

The chi-square test does not rely on assumptions about data distribution, making it suitable for non-normal datasets.

2. **Flexibility**

It can analyze relationships in various fields, including healthcare, marketing, education, and social sciences.

3. **Easy to Compute and Interpret**

The calculations are straightforward, and the results provide clear insights into the presence or absence of relationships.

4. **Applicable to Large Datasets**

The chi-square test is particularly effective when analyzing large datasets with multiple categories.

Limitations of the Chi-Square Test

1. **Sensitive to Sample Size**

The test requires a sufficiently large sample size to ensure that expected frequencies are reliable. Small sample sizes may lead to inaccurate results.

2. **Assumes Independence**

The chi-square test assumes that observations are independent. Violations of this assumption can invalidate the results.

3. **Cannot Measure Strength**

While the test identifies the existence of a relationship, it does not measure the strength or direction of the association.

4. **Ineffective for Sparse Data**

If expected frequencies are too low (less than 5), the test may not be valid. In such cases, Fisher's exact test is a better alternative.

5. **Limited to Categorical Variables**

The test cannot be used for continuous variables, such as income or height, which require other statistical methods like regression or ANOVA.

Practical Example of a Chi-Square Test

Scenario: A retailer wants to know if customer gender influences product preference (smartphones vs. laptops).

1. **Data Collection**: Record observed frequencies in a contingency table:

Gender	Smartphones	Laptops	Total
Male	50	30	80
Female	40	60	100
Total	90	90	180

2. **Expected Frequencies**: Calculate expected frequencies for each cell:
For males purchasing smartphones:

$$E = \frac{(80 \times 90)}{180} = 40$$

Similarly, calculate expected frequencies for all other cells.

3. **Chi-Square Calculation**: Compare observed and expected frequencies using the formula:

$$\chi^2 = \sum \frac{(O - E)^2}{E}$$

Compute for all cells and sum the values to find χ^2.

4. **Result Interpretation**: Compare the calculated χ^2 with the critical value for 1 degree of freedom (df = (rows - 1) × (columns - 1)) at a 0.05 significance level. If χ^2>critical value, gender significantly influences product preference.

Applications of the Chi-Square Test

1. **Healthcare**

   - Examining whether patient gender is associated with treatment preferences.
   - Testing relationships between smoking habits (yes/no) and disease prevalence.

2. **Marketing**

   - Analyzing if age group influences preferred product categories.
   - Testing whether location affects brand preferences.

3. **Education**

   ○ Determining if student performance (pass/fail) is influenced by teaching methods.

4. **Social Sciences**

   ○ Examining whether socioeconomic status affects voting patterns.

5. **Quality Control**

   ○ Identifying whether defects in manufacturing are related to shifts or machine operators.

The chi-square test is an essential tool for analyzing categorical data, providing insights into relationships between variables. While it is straightforward and versatile, researchers must ensure that sample sizes are adequate and assumptions are met for valid results. Properly applied, the chi-square test offers powerful evidence to inform decisions across fields.

Steps in Data Analysis

1. **Data Cleaning**: Eliminate duplicates, fix missing values, and ensure consistency.
2. **Organize Data**: Structure data in tables for clarity and ease of analysis.
3. **Select Tools**: Choose software like SPSS, R, or Excel based on data type and research goals.
4. **Apply Analytical Techniques**: Use appropriate methods for analysis (e.g., regression, thematic analysis).
5. **Visualize Data**: Present findings using bar charts, scatterplots, or thematic maps for better understanding.

Tools for Data Analysis

- **Excel**: User-friendly for basic statistics and charts.
- **SPSS**: Preferred for advanced statistical tests.
- **R**: Open-source software for handling large datasets and complex models.

This chapter has equipped you with a detailed understanding of data analysis techniques. By knowing **why**, **when**, and **how** to use these tools, you can confidently analyze data, draw actionable insights, and make impactful contributions to your field.

Statistical Techniques for Data Analysis

Statistical techniques are essential for interpreting data and drawing meaningful conclusions. These techniques enable researchers to identify relationships, test hypotheses, and validate findings with precision and accuracy.

1. Analysis of Variance (ANOVA)

ANOVA is a statistical method used to compare the means of three or more groups to determine if there is a significant difference among them.

Applications:

- Comparing the effectiveness of different marketing campaigns.

- Evaluating student performance across different teaching methods.

Example in India:
A company like Hindustan Unilever might use ANOVA to compare sales performance across three regions: North, South, and West.
Steps in ANOVA:

1. Define the null hypothesis (H^0): All group means are equal.
2. Calculate between-group and within-group variances.
3. Determine the F-ratio to test the hypothesis.
4. Reject or fail to reject H^0 based on the significance level (p-value).

2. Regression Analysis
Regression is used to understand the relationship between dependent and independent variables. It predicts outcomes and evaluates the impact of variables.
Types of Regression:

1. **Linear Regression:**
   Examines the relationship between two variables.

   ○ **Example:** Studying how advertising expenditure impacts sales in Flipkart.

2. **Multiple Regression:**
   Analyzes the effect of multiple independent variables on a dependent variable.

   ○ **Example in India:** A bank might study how interest rates, income levels, and customer age influence loan approval rates.

3. Chi-Square Test
The Chi-Square test is used for categorical data to determine if there is a significant association between two variables.
Applications:

- Testing customer preferences across product categories.
- Examining relationships between demographic factors and voting behavior.

Example in India:
A retailer like Big Bazaar might use the Chi-Square test to analyze whether customer preferences for product categories vary by age group.
4. T-Test
A t-test compares the means of two groups to identify if the difference is statistically significant.
Types of T-Tests:

1. **Independent Sample T-Test:**
   Compares two independent groups.

   ○ **Example:** Comparing online shopping behavior between men and women.

2. **Paired Sample T-Test:**
   Compares two measurements from the same group.

   - **Example in India:** Measuring employee productivity before and after a training program in Wipro.

5. Correlation Analysis

Correlation measures the strength and direction of the relationship between two variables.
Types:

- **Positive Correlation:** Both variables increase or decrease together.
- **Negative Correlation:** One variable increases as the other decreases.

Example in India:
Analyzing the correlation between rainfall and agricultural productivity in Punjab.

6. Factor Analysis

Factor analysis reduces a large number of variables into smaller factors to simplify data interpretation.
Example in India:
A market research firm might use factor analysis to identify underlying factors influencing customer loyalty.

7. Cluster Analysis

Cluster analysis groups similar data points into clusters based on shared characteristics.
Example in India:
E-commerce platforms like Amazon use clustering to segment customers based on purchasing behavior.

8. Time Series Analysis

Time series analysis examines data points collected over time to identify trends, seasonal effects, and patterns.
Example in India:
Analyzing monthly inflation rates in India to forecast economic trends.

Steps for Applying Statistical Techniques

1. **Define Objectives:**
   Identify the research question or hypothesis.
2. **Select Appropriate Tools:**
   Match statistical techniques with data type and research objectives.
3. **Prepare Data:**
   Clean and organize data for analysis.
4. **Perform Analysis:**
   Use software tools like SPSS, R, or Python for calculations.
5. **Interpret Results:**
   Evaluate outcomes in the context of research objectives.

Importance of Statistical Techniques

1. **Supports Decision-Making:**
   Provides evidence-based insights for business and policy decisions.
2. **Validates Hypotheses:**
   Confirms or refutes assumptions with statistical rigor.
3. **Identifies Relationships:**
   Reveals correlations and causal links between variables.

4. **Forecasting:**
Enables predictions for future trends and outcomes.

Real-World Applications in India

1. **Elections:**
Exit poll agencies use regression and correlation to predict voting trends.
2. **Healthcare:**
Hospitals use statistical tools to analyze patient recovery rates and treatment efficacy.
3. **Agriculture:**
Time series analysis is employed to study crop production patterns over decades.

Statistical techniques form the backbone of data analysis, ensuring that research findings are robust, reliable, and actionable. Whether it's understanding consumer behavior, testing the impact of policies, or forecasting trends, these tools enable researchers to navigate data complexities and extract valuable insights.

References

Creswell, J. W. (2014). *Research design: Qualitative, quantitative, and mixed methods approaches* (4th ed.). Sage Publications.
Kothari, C. R. (2004). *Research methodology: Methods and techniques.* New Age International.
Tabachnick, B. G., & Fidell, L. S. (2019). *Using multivariate statistics* (7th ed.). Pearson Education.

CHAPTER IX

Reporting and Presenting Research Findings

Priya, a social science researcher, completed an extensive study on the impact of microfinance programs on women's empowerment in rural India. While her findings were robust, her report failed to communicate them effectively to policymakers and NGOs. Her overly technical language, lack of visual aids, and unstructured presentation left her audience confused.

Her mentor suggested revising her report by focusing on clarity, including visuals like charts and graphs, and tailoring her presentation to the audience's needs. When she presented the revised report, policymakers praised its actionable insights and clarity.

Priya's experience highlights the importance of presenting research findings in a way that is both clear and impactful. This chapter focuses on how to effectively report and present research findings, ensuring they make a meaningful impact on your intended audience.

Importance of Reporting and Presentation

1. **Conveys the Research Message**

   - A well-structured report ensures that the research objectives, methods, and findings are clearly communicated.
   - Example: A report on customer satisfaction highlights key drivers like service quality and pricing.

2. **Facilitates Decision-Making**

   - Findings presented in actionable terms enable organizations, policymakers, or stakeholders to make informed decisions.
   - Example: A public health report linking clean water access to reduced disease rates helps design targeted interventions.

3. **Engages the Audience**

   - Effective use of visuals, summaries, and straightforward language keeps readers or listeners engaged.

4. **Establishes Credibility**

   - A well-documented and professionally presented report enhances the researcher's reputation and the reliability of the findings.

5. **Enables Knowledge Sharing**

   - Published reports and presentations contribute to the larger body of knowledge, allowing others to build on your work.

Types of Research Reports

1. **Academic Research Reports**

   - Prepared for academic audiences, including theses, dissertations, or journal articles.
   - Example: A thesis on the impact of leadership styles on employee motivation.

2. **Technical Reports**

   - Focused on technical details, often prepared for experts in the field.
   - Example: A report on machine learning algorithms for predicting stock prices.

3. **Policy Reports**

   - Tailored for policymakers, focusing on actionable insights and recommendations.
   - Example: A report recommending strategies to increase rural literacy rates.

4. **Business Reports**

   - Designed for organizational stakeholders, focusing on practical outcomes.
   - Example: A market research report analyzing customer preferences for a new product.

5. **General Audience Reports**

   - Simplified reports for the public, emphasizing key findings and their implications.
   - Example: A report summarizing climate change impacts for a community audience.

Ingredients of a Research Report

A well-structured research report is essential for communicating findings effectively to various stakeholders, including academic peers, policymakers, or business leaders. Each section of the report serves a specific purpose, ensuring clarity, coherence, and logical flow.

Key Components of a Research Report

1. **Title Page**
   The title page provides essential information about the report, including:

   - Title of the study
   - Name of the researcher(s)
   - Institutional affiliation
   - Date of submission

   Example:
   Title: "The Impact of Digital Payments on Rural Economies in India: A Study of Maharashtra"

1. **Abstract**

   The abstract offers a concise summary of the research, including the problem, methodology, key findings, and conclusions. It helps readers decide whether to delve deeper into the report.

   Tips for Writing:

   - Limit to 250–300 words.
   - Highlight the purpose, methods, results, and implications.

3. **Table of Contents**

   A clear and detailed table of contents helps readers navigate the report efficiently. It includes major headings and subheadings with corresponding page numbers.

4. **Introduction**

   The introduction sets the stage by presenting the research problem, objectives, and significance of the study. It also outlines the structure of the report.

   Key Elements:

   - Background and context of the study
   - Statement of the problem
   - Research objectives and hypotheses
   - Scope and limitations

   Example:

In a report on e-commerce adoption in India, the introduction might describe the rapid growth of online marketplaces and their challenges in rural areas.

5. **Literature Review**

   This section provides a review of existing studies, theories, and frameworks relevant to the research problem. It identifies gaps and establishes the study's contribution to the field.

   Example in India:

A literature review on renewable energy adoption might discuss policies like the Jawaharlal Nehru National Solar Mission.

6. **Methodology**

   The methodology explains how the research was conducted, ensuring transparency and replicability.

   Key Details:

   - Research design (e.g., descriptive, experimental)
   - Sampling techniques and sample size
   - Data collection methods (e.g., surveys, interviews)
   - Tools and techniques for data analysis

   Example:

A study on workplace stress might describe using stratified sampling to select participants across various industries.

7. **Results and Findings**
   This section presents the data in an organized manner, often using tables, charts, and graphs. Findings should be clearly linked to the research objectives.

   Example:
   In a study on mobile banking usage, findings might show a significant correlation between literacy levels and app adoption rates.

8. **Discussion and Interpretation**
   The discussion interprets the results in the context of the research objectives and existing literature. It explains the implications of the findings and addresses any unexpected outcomes.

   Example:
   A study on telemedicine adoption might discuss how cultural barriers influence patient preferences, despite high internet penetration.

9. **Conclusion and Recommendations**
   The conclusion summarizes the study, emphasizing key findings and their implications. Recommendations provide actionable steps for stakeholders.

   Example in India:
   A report on agricultural technology might recommend subsidizing IoT-based solutions to improve crop monitoring.

10. **References/Bibliography**
    This section lists all sources cited in the report, following a specific citation style (e.g., APA, MLA).

    Example:

    - Creswell, J. W. (2014). *Research design: Qualitative, quantitative, and mixed methods approaches* (4th ed.). Sage Publications.

11. **Appendices**
    Appendices include supplementary material, such as raw data, survey instruments, or detailed calculations, that supports the main report.

Importance of a Well-Structured Research Report

1. **Clarity and Readability:**
   A structured report ensures that complex findings are presented in a clear and logical sequence.
2. **Credibility:**
   Detailed documentation of methods and findings enhances the report's validity.
3. **Actionability:**
   Well-crafted recommendations help stakeholders make informed decisions.

Real-World Example of Research Reports in India

1. **NITI Aayog's Policy Reports:**
   These reports often include comprehensive sections on background, methodology, and actionable

recommendations for sustainable development.

2. **Market Research by Nielsen India:**
   Nielsen's reports on consumer behavior typically use clear visuals, executive summaries, and appendices for detailed data.

Structure of a Research Report

A research report typically follows a standardized structure:

1. Title Page

- Includes the title, author(s), institution, and date.
- Example: **"The Role of Social Media in Shaping Political Awareness Among Indian Youth"**.

2. Abstract

- A concise summary of the research problem, methods, findings, and conclusions.
- Example: "This study explores how social media influences political awareness among Indian youth, finding that platforms like Twitter and Instagram play a critical role."

3. Introduction

- Provides background, defines the research problem, and states objectives.
- Example: Explaining the rising influence of social media in shaping political opinions.

4. Literature Review

- Summarizes existing research, identifies gaps, and connects them to your study.

5. Methodology

- Details the research design, sampling techniques, and data collection methods.
- Example: Using a survey of 1,000 respondents aged 18–30 to measure political awareness.

6. Results

- Presents the findings using text, tables, and visuals.

7. Discussion

- Interprets results, linking them back to research objectives and hypotheses.
- Example: Discussing how social media usage correlates with increased political engagement.

8. Conclusion and Recommendations

- Summarizes findings and suggests actions or future research directions.
- Example: Recommending digital literacy programs to promote informed political discussions online.

9. References

- Lists all sources cited in the report. Use a standard citation style like APA or MLA.

10. Appendices

- Includes additional materials like questionnaires, raw data, or detailed calculations.

Presentation of Research Findings

Tips for Effective Presentation

1. **Know Your Audience**

   - Tailor content to your audience's expertise and interests.
   - Example: Use technical terms for academic audiences but simplify language for policymakers.

2. **Use Visual Aids**

   - Incorporate graphs, charts, and infographics to summarize data.
   - Example: A bar chart comparing literacy rates across regions.

3. **Organize Content Logically**

   - Follow a clear structure: introduction, main findings, and conclusion.

4. **Keep It Concise**

   ○ Focus on key points and avoid unnecessary details.

5. **Engage Your Audience**

   ○ Use stories, examples, or questions to make the presentation interactive.
   ○ Example: Start with a compelling story about an individual affected by the research topic.

Tools for Presenting Research

1. **Microsoft PowerPoint**: For creating slideshows.
2. **Canva**: For designing visually appealing presentations.
3. **Tableau**: For interactive data visualizations.
4. **Prezi**: For creating dynamic, non-linear presentations.

Common Mistakes in Reporting and Presentation

1. **Overloading Slides with Text**

   ○ Solution: Use bullet points and visuals to summarize key ideas.

2. **Failing to Highlight Key Findings**

   ○ Solution: Emphasize actionable insights in the conclusion and executive summary.

3. **Using Complex Jargon**

   ○ Solution: Simplify language for non-expert audiences.

4. **Ignoring Visual Design**

   ○ Solution: Use consistent fonts, colors, and layouts for a professional appearance.

5. **Lack of Engagement**

   ○ Solution: Ask questions or share anecdotes to connect with the audience.

Real-World Application: Reporting Research on Remote Work

Research Problem: How has remote work impacted employee productivity during the COVID-19 pandemic?

1. **Title**: "Remote Work and Productivity: A Study of IT Employees in India"

2. **Abstract**: Summarizes the study's focus on flexibility, work-life balance, and productivity metrics.
3. **Findings**:

   ◦ Remote work improved productivity for 60% of employees.
   ◦ Work-life balance issues negatively impacted 25% of employees.

4. **Recommendations**:

   ◦ Employers should offer flexible schedules and mental health support programs.

5. **Presentation**:

   ◦ Pie charts showing productivity metrics.
   ◦ Infographics on challenges faced by employees.

Reporting and presenting research findings is as critical as conducting the research itself. By structuring your report effectively, using visuals, and tailoring your presentation to your audience, you can ensure your research makes a meaningful impact. In the next chapter, we will explore research ethics, focusing on the principles and practices that safeguard the integrity and credibility of your work.

References

Bell, J. (2014). *Doing your research project: A guide for first-time researchers.* McGraw-Hill Education.

Creswell, J. W. (2014). *Research design: Qualitative, quantitative, and mixed methods approaches* (4th ed.). Sage Publications.

Kothari, C. R. (2004). *Research methodology: Methods and techniques.* New Age International.

Neuman, W. L. (2014). *Social research methods: Qualitative and quantitative approaches* (7th ed.). Pearson Education.

Zikmund, W. G., Babin, B. J., Carr, J. C., & Griffin, M. (2013). *Business research methods.* Cengage Learning.

CHAPTER X

Research Ethics

Ananya, a postgraduate researcher, was studying the mental health challenges faced by adolescents in urban schools. Excited to gather data, she created a questionnaire and began distributing it to students without considering ethical guidelines. Soon, she faced backlash from parents and teachers, who were concerned about the personal nature of the questions and the lack of consent.

Her research supervisor intervened and explained the importance of **ethics** in research—how ensuring privacy, obtaining informed consent, and safeguarding participant well-being are paramount. With this knowledge, Ananya redesigned her study, prioritizing ethical considerations, and gained the trust of her participants.

This chapter delves into the principles and practices of research ethics, helping you understand how to conduct research responsibly and maintain the integrity of your study.

What is Research Ethics?

Definition

Research ethics refers to a set of moral principles and standards that guide researchers to conduct studies responsibly, ensuring fairness, integrity, and respect for all stakeholders.

According to Bryman (2015), "Research ethics is concerned with the ethical principles guiding the research process, from inception to publication, particularly in relation to the rights and welfare of participants."

Importance of Research Ethics

1. **Protects Participant Rights**

   - Ensures that participants are treated with dignity, respect, and care.
   - Example: Avoiding sensitive questions that could cause psychological distress to respondents.

2. **Enhances Credibility and Validity**

   - Ethical research practices build trust and ensure findings are credible.
   - Example: Transparent reporting of methods and results avoids accusations of misconduct.

3. **Promotes Social Responsibility**

   - Ensures that research contributes positively to society and avoids harm.
   - Example: Avoiding biased interpretations that could perpetuate stereotypes.

4. **Prevents Legal and Professional Repercussions**

   - Adhering to ethical guidelines helps researchers avoid lawsuits or penalties.

5. **Upholds Integrity in Academia**

○ Ethical conduct reinforces the value of honesty and transparency in research.

Principles of Research Ethics

1. Informed Consent

- **Definition**: Participants must voluntarily agree to participate after being fully informed about the study's purpose, methods, risks, and benefits.
- **Key Practices**:

  1. Provide participants with a clear and comprehensive consent form.
  2. Ensure consent is obtained in writing or through recorded verbal agreement.
  3. Allow participants to withdraw from the study at any time without consequences.

- **Example**: A researcher studying workplace stress explains to employees that their data will remain confidential and obtains signed consent forms before starting interviews.

2. Confidentiality and Privacy

- **Definition**: Researchers must protect participants' personal information and ensure it is not disclosed without consent.
- **Key Practices**:

  1. Anonymize data by removing identifying details like names or contact information.
  2. Use secure storage systems for digital and physical data.
  3. Share data only with authorized personnel involved in the research.

- **Example**: In a study on mental health, researchers use pseudonyms for participants and store responses in encrypted files.

3. Avoidance of Harm

- **Definition**: Researchers must ensure their study does not cause physical, emotional, or psychological harm to participants.
- **Key Practices**:

  1. Conduct a risk assessment to identify potential harms and mitigate them.
  2. Avoid asking intrusive or distressing questions without a clear purpose.
  3. Provide participants access to resources or support if distress occurs.

- **Example**: A sociologist studying survivors of domestic violence ensures that interviews are conducted in a safe and supportive environment, with counselors on standby.

4. Honesty and Transparency

- **Definition**: Researchers must present their methods, data, and findings truthfully, avoiding fabrication, falsification, or selective reporting.
- **Key Practices**:

  1. Report all findings, including unexpected or negative results.
  2. Avoid manipulating data to fit preconceived conclusions.
  3. Disclose any conflicts of interest.

- **Example**: A researcher studying the effect of a new teaching method reports that the results were inconclusive, instead of selectively presenting positive outcomes.

5. Justice and Fairness

- **Definition**: Ensure fair treatment of all participants and avoid exploiting vulnerable groups.
- **Key Practices**:

  1. Avoid overburdening specific populations, such as minorities or economically disadvantaged groups.
  2. Ensure equitable distribution of research benefits.
  3. Include diverse participants to avoid biased outcomes.

- **Example**: In a study on healthcare accessibility, the researcher ensures that participants include individuals from both urban and rural areas.

Ethical Considerations in Data Collection

1. **Cultural Sensitivity**

   - Respect cultural norms and values when designing surveys or interviews.
   - Example: In a study involving indigenous communities, researchers seek input from community leaders before collecting data.

2. **Deception**

   - Avoid misleading participants unless justified and approved by an ethics board.
   - Example: A researcher studying behavior under false assumptions debriefs participants afterward.

3. **Use of Incentives**

- Ensure incentives are reasonable and do not coerce participation.
- Example: Offering a token gift to participants in a survey on consumer preferences.

4. **Third-Party Data Use**

- Obtain permission to use secondary data and ensure compliance with privacy laws.
- Example: Using anonymized hospital records for public health research after receiving approval from relevant authorities.

Ethical Review Boards

Many institutions have ethical review boards or institutional review boards (IRBs) that assess the ethical aspects of research proposals.

1. **Role of IRBs**

- Review and approve research designs to ensure compliance with ethical standards.
- Monitor ongoing studies for ethical adherence.

2. **How to Apply**

- Submit a detailed proposal outlining objectives, methods, and ethical considerations.
- Include informed consent forms, risk assessments, and data management plans.

Consequences of Ethical Violations

1. **Loss of Credibility**

- Unethical practices can damage a researcher's reputation and career.

2. **Legal Repercussions**

- Violating laws related to privacy or consent can lead to lawsuits or fines.

3. **Harm to Participants**

- Breaches of confidentiality or causing distress can have serious consequences for individuals.

4. **Retraction of Published Work**

- Journals may retract papers if ethical violations are discovered.

Real-World Application: Ethical Research in Action

Case Study: Studying Access to Education for Girls in Rural India

1. **Ethical Considerations:**

   - Obtaining consent from parents and community leaders.
   - Ensuring questions are culturally appropriate and non-intrusive.
   - Providing anonymized responses to stakeholders.

2. **Outcome:**

   - The study highlights barriers like early marriage and lack of facilities while maintaining participants' dignity and trust.

Ethics are the foundation of responsible research, ensuring participant rights, integrity, and societal benefit. By adhering to ethical principles like informed consent, confidentiality, and honesty, researchers can conduct impactful studies while maintaining trust and credibility. In the next chapter, we will explore advanced research techniques and emerging methodologies, equipping you to address complex problems with innovative approaches.

Ethical Considerations in Research

Ethical considerations form the backbone of any credible research study. They ensure the protection of participants, the integrity of the research process, and the validity of findings. Adhering to ethical principles not only safeguards the interests of all stakeholders but also enhances the trustworthiness of the study.

Key Ethical Principles in Research

1. **Informed Consent**
   Researchers must ensure that participants are fully aware of the study's purpose, procedures, potential risks, and their rights. Participants must voluntarily agree to take part without coercion.

   - **Application in India:**
     In a healthcare study on rural vaccination programs, researchers should explain the study's intent in local languages and obtain signed or verbal consent.

1. **Confidentiality and Privacy**
   Protecting participants' personal information is paramount. Data should be anonymized to prevent identification and unauthorized access.

   - **Example:**
     A survey on LGBTQ+ workplace inclusion in India must ensure that participants' identities are protected, especially in sensitive contexts.

3. **Avoiding Harm**
   Research must prioritize the well-being of participants, ensuring that no physical, psychological, or emotional harm occurs during or after the study.

   - **Example in India:**
     In a study on mental health awareness, researchers should avoid triggering questions or use professional support for participants if distress arises.

4. **Voluntary Participation**
Participation must always be voluntary, with individuals having the right to withdraw from the study at any point without penalty.

- ◦ **Example:**
  A market research study on food delivery services must allow respondents to exit surveys without repercussions.

5. **Honesty and Transparency**
Researchers must report findings truthfully, avoiding fabrication, falsification, or selective omission of data.

- ◦ **Example:**
  A company conducting internal employee satisfaction surveys must report findings transparently, even if results highlight managerial shortcomings.

6. **Avoiding Conflict of Interest**
Researchers must disclose any potential conflicts of interest, such as funding sources or affiliations, that could bias the study.

- ◦ **Example:**
  A pharmaceutical company funding research on its own products must ensure independent oversight to avoid biased results.

7. **Proper Use of Data**
Data collected during the study should only be used for the stated research purposes. Misuse of data violates ethical guidelines and can harm participants or other stakeholders.

- ◦ **Example:**
  A survey on online shopping habits in India should not sell respondents' data to third parties without explicit consent.

Special Considerations in Indian Context

1. **Cultural Sensitivity:**
India's diverse cultural and linguistic landscape necessitates culturally appropriate research practices. Researchers should adapt survey instruments and methodologies to local contexts.

- ◦ **Example:**
  In rural studies, researchers might need to involve community leaders or use culturally relevant analogies to explain the study's purpose.

2. **Vulnerable Populations:**
Extra care must be taken when researching children, economically disadvantaged groups, or individuals with disabilities.

- ◦ **Example:**
  In a study on child nutrition, researchers must seek parental or guardian consent and ensure that the study poses no risk to children.

3. **Government and Institutional Guidelines:**
Research in India often requires compliance with ethical guidelines issued by bodies such as the Indian Council of Medical Research (ICMR) or university ethics boards.

Steps to Ensure Ethical Compliance

1. **Obtain Ethical Approval:**
Seek approval from relevant ethics committees before initiating research, especially for studies involving human subjects.
2. **Develop Consent Forms:**
Include clear, jargon-free explanations of the study's objectives, risks, and benefits.
3. **Anonymize Data:**
Use coding systems to ensure participant anonymity.
4. **Monitor Ongoing Compliance:**
Regularly review research practices to address any emerging ethical concerns.

Real-World Applications of Ethics in Indian Research

1. **Clinical Trials:**
Pharmaceutical trials in India adhere to Good Clinical Practice (GCP) guidelines to protect participants and ensure transparent reporting.
2. **Policy Studies:**
Government-led research on urbanization issues must involve ethical consultations to ensure unbiased and actionable findings.
3. **Market Research:**
Companies like Nielsen ensure that data collected from Indian consumers is anonymized and used solely for the stated research objectives.

Ethical considerations are integral to the success and credibility of any research study. By prioritizing informed consent, confidentiality, and cultural sensitivity, researchers can ensure that their work contributes positively to the field while respecting the rights and dignity of participants. In India, where cultural, socio-economic, and linguistic diversity adds layers of complexity, adherence to ethical principles becomes even more critical.

References

Beauchamp, T. L., & Childress, J. F. (2013). *Principles of biomedical ethics*. Oxford University Press.

Bryman, A. (2015). *Social research methods* (5th ed.). Oxford University Press.

Emanuel, E. J., Wendler, D., & Grady, C. (2000). What makes clinical research ethical? *JAMA*, 283(20), 2701–2711.

Flick, U. (2018). *An introduction to qualitative research*. SAGE Publications.

Israel, M., & Hay, I. (2006). *Research ethics for social scientists: Between ethical conduct and regulatory compliance*. SAGE Publications.

Resnik, D. B. (2020). *The ethics of science: An introduction*. Routledge.

Shamoo, A. E., & Resnik, D. B. (2015). *Responsible conduct of research*. Oxford University Press.

Sieber, J. E. (2009). *Planning ethically responsible research*. SAGE Publications.

CHAPTER XI

Advanced Research Techniques and Emerging Methodologies

Vikram, a doctoral researcher, was struggling with his study on the impact of social media influencers on consumer purchasing decisions. Traditional survey methods provided some insights, but they lacked the depth to understand how specific algorithms amplified influencer content. A peer suggested exploring **netnography**, a qualitative technique for studying online communities, and **machine learning** to analyze massive datasets from social media platforms.

By combining these advanced methodologies, Vikram gained valuable insights into both consumer behavior and the digital platforms' role in shaping it. His innovative approach added depth to his study and set a benchmark for others.

This chapter introduces advanced research techniques and emerging methodologies that enable researchers to tackle complex problems, especially in the rapidly evolving fields of social sciences and management.

What Are Advanced Research Techniques?

Definition

Advanced research techniques involve sophisticated methods and tools designed to handle complex research questions, large datasets, and multidisciplinary challenges. These techniques often combine traditional research methods with technological innovations.

Importance

1. **Addresses Complex Problems**

   ◦ Advanced techniques handle multi-layered problems, such as analyzing social networks or predicting market trends.

2. **Enhances Accuracy**

   ◦ Tools like artificial intelligence (AI) and machine learning improve the precision of data analysis.

3. **Supports Big Data**

   ◦ Techniques like sentiment analysis and data mining can process large datasets efficiently.

4. **Facilitates Multidisciplinary Research**

   ◦ Combines knowledge from different fields to offer holistic solutions.

5. **Keeps Research Relevant**

   ◦ Emerging methodologies align with technological advancements, ensuring research stays up-to-date.

Emerging Methodologies in Social Sciences and Management

1. Netnography

- **Definition**: A qualitative research method that studies online communities and cultures. Developed by Kozinets (2015), netnography adapts ethnographic techniques for digital platforms.
- **Application**:

  1. Understanding customer reviews on e-commerce sites.
  2. Analyzing discourse on social media about climate change.

- **Steps**:

  1. Define the research question and identify relevant online communities.
  2. Collect data from discussions, posts, and interactions.
  3. Analyze themes, behaviors, and patterns.

- **Example**: Studying how online fitness communities motivate members to adopt healthier lifestyles.

2. Machine Learning in Research

- **Definition**: A branch of AI that uses algorithms to identify patterns in data and make predictions or decisions without explicit programming.
- **Application**:

  1. Sentiment analysis of tweets about a brand.
  2. Predicting employee turnover using HR data.

- **Steps**:

  1. Preprocess data by cleaning and organizing it.
  2. Train machine learning models using labeled datasets.
  3. Test and validate models for accuracy.

- **Example**: Using machine learning to identify key factors influencing student performance based on school datasets.

  Tools:

- Python libraries like TensorFlow and Scikit-learn.
- Software like RapidMiner.

3. Mixed-Methods Research with Integration

- **Definition**: A methodological approach that combines qualitative and quantitative data, emphasizing integration for richer insights.
- **Application**:

  1. Studying employee satisfaction through surveys (quantitative) and interviews (qualitative).
  2. Evaluating the impact of government policies using statistics and case studies.

- **Steps**:

  1. Identify the research problem and decide on the qualitative-quantitative balance.
  2. Collect data using both methods simultaneously or sequentially.
  3. Integrate findings during analysis and interpretation.

- **Example**: Combining survey data with focus group discussions to study the effects of remote work on productivity.

4. Social Network Analysis (SNA)

- **Definition**: A technique for mapping and analyzing relationships and interactions within networks, such as social groups or organizations.
- **Application**:

  1. Analyzing employee collaboration within organizations.
  2. Mapping influencers' roles in online marketing campaigns.

- **Steps**:

  1. Define the network and data sources (e.g., social media, organizational charts).
  2. Collect data on nodes (individuals) and edges (relationships).
  3. Analyze metrics like centrality and density to understand the network structure.

- **Example**: Mapping interactions within a team to identify communication bottlenecks.

  Tools:

- Gephi, UCINET, and Python's NetworkX library.

5. Sentiment Analysis

- **Definition**: Uses natural language processing (NLP) to identify emotions and opinions expressed in text data.
- **Application**:

1. Assessing public sentiment about new policies using social media data.
2. Analyzing customer reviews to improve products.

- **Steps:**

1. Preprocess text data by removing noise (e.g., hashtags, emojis).
2. Use NLP tools to classify sentiments (positive, negative, neutral).
3. Visualize trends using graphs or heatmaps.

- **Example**: Analyzing tweets to gauge public opinion about a new budget proposal.

    Tools:

- Python's NLTK and TextBlob libraries.
- Commercial platforms like IBM Watson.

6. Case Study Research with Simulation

- **Definition**: Combines real-world case studies with simulated models to test scenarios and predict outcomes.
- **Application:**

1. Studying disaster management strategies using simulated data.
2. Analyzing market responses to product launches using business simulations.

- **Steps:**

1. Select a real-world case relevant to the research question.
2. Develop a simulation model based on observed data.
3. Test different scenarios to predict outcomes.

- **Example**: Simulating the impact of increased social media advertising on sales using historical data from a case study.

Challenges of Advanced Techniques

1. **Technical Expertise**

   - Many methods require programming skills or specialized knowledge.
   - Solution: Collaborate with experts or take training courses.

2. **Cost and Resources**

   - Advanced tools can be expensive and resource-intensive.
   - Solution: Use open-source tools like Python or R for cost-effective analysis.

3. **Data Privacy Concerns**

    - Collecting and analyzing large datasets raises ethical concerns.
    - Solution: Anonymize data and follow data protection regulations like GDPR.

4. **Integration Complexity**

    - Combining different methodologies can lead to inconsistencies.
    - Solution: Plan integration during the research design phase.

Real-World Application

Case Study: Social Media Influencers and Consumer Behavior

Objective: To analyze how influencers shape purchasing decisions.
   Methods:

1. **Netnography**: Study comments and interactions on influencer posts.
2. **Sentiment Analysis**: Analyze follower sentiments in comments using NLP.
3. **SNA**: Map the influencer's network to identify key nodes and interactions.

Outcome: Identified that influencers with high engagement rates and genuine connections drive more purchases. Advanced research techniques and emerging methodologies provide powerful tools for addressing complex problems in social sciences and management. By adopting approaches like netnography, machine learning, and sentiment analysis, researchers can generate richer, more actionable insights. The next chapter will explore the future of research in a globalized, technology-driven world, highlighting trends and opportunities for innovation.

Visual Representation of Data

Effective data visualization bridges the gap between complex datasets and actionable insights. By translating numerical and textual data into graphical formats, researchers can enhance comprehension, highlight key trends, and support evidence-based decision-making.
   Common Types of Visual Data Representations

1. **Tables**
    Tables organize raw data into rows and columns for easy reference and comparison. They are particularly useful for presenting large datasets with specific values.

    Example in India:
A table showing the literacy rates across Indian states over the last decade can highlight disparities and progress.

1. **Bar Charts**
    Bar charts use rectangular bars to compare different categories of data. They are ideal for showing comparisons and distributions.

Example:

A bar chart comparing monthly sales figures for Flipkart, Amazon, and Snapdeal during the festive season.

3. **Pie Charts**

   Pie charts illustrate proportions or percentages of a whole, making them suitable for displaying categorical data.

   Example in India:

A pie chart showing the market share of telecom providers like Jio, Airtel, and Vodafone Idea.

4. **Line Graphs**

   Line graphs depict trends over time by connecting data points with a continuous line. They are effective for illustrating patterns and changes.

   Example:

A line graph tracking the number of internet users in India from 2010 to 2023.

5. **Histograms**

   Histograms resemble bar charts but are used for frequency distributions of continuous data.

   Example:

A histogram showing the distribution of household incomes in urban India.

6. **Scatter Plots**

   Scatter plots reveal relationships or correlations between two variables by plotting data points on an X-Y axis.

   Example:

A scatter plot showing the relationship between rainfall levels and crop yields in Maharashtra.

7. **Heat Maps**

   Heat maps use color gradients to represent data density or intensity. They are often used in geographic or spatial analysis.

   Example in India:

A heat map showing COVID-19 case density across Indian states during the pandemic.

8. **Bubble Charts**

   Bubble charts add a third dimension to scatter plots by varying the size of the bubbles to represent an additional variable.

   Example:

A bubble chart comparing GDP (bubble size), literacy rate, and population of Indian states.

   Best Practices for Data Visualization

1. **Choose the Right Chart Type:**

   Ensure the visualization matches the type of data and the intended message. For example, use a bar chart for comparisons and a line graph for trends.

2. **Simplify the Design:**

   Avoid cluttered visuals by limiting the number of data points and focusing on key insights. Minimalist designs improve readability.

3. **Use Color Strategically:**
Colors should differentiate data points clearly without overwhelming the viewer. For instance, in pie charts, use distinct colors for each segment.

4. **Label Axes and Legends Clearly:**
Axes, titles, and legends must be descriptive and concise, ensuring that viewers can understand the chart without additional explanations.

5. **Highlight Key Insights:**
Use annotations, bolding, or different colors to draw attention to critical data points or trends.

Tools for Data Visualization

1. **Microsoft Excel:**
Widely used for creating basic charts and graphs.

2. **Tableau:**
Advanced software for creating interactive and complex visualizations.

3. **Google Data Studio:**
Ideal for connecting and visualizing data from multiple sources.

4. **Power BI:**
A robust tool for building dynamic dashboards and reports.

5. **R and Python:**
Libraries like ggplot2 (R) and matplotlib (Python) enable customized visualizations for advanced analytics.

Importance of Data Visualization in Research

1. **Enhances Comprehension:**
Visuals simplify complex data, making it easier for readers to grasp the findings.

2. **Identifies Patterns and Trends:**
Graphical representations reveal insights that might be overlooked in raw data.

3. **Supports Decision-Making:**
Stakeholders can make informed decisions based on clear, evidence-backed visuals.

4. **Improves Engagement:**
Readers are more likely to stay engaged with visually appealing data presentations.

Real-World Applications in India

1. **E-Governance:**
Platforms like MyGov use data dashboards to visualize citizen feedback on government schemes.

2. **Education Sector:**
Reports from CBSE use charts to show trends in student performance over the years.

3. **Financial Research:**
SEBI's annual reports include visualizations of stock market trends, investment flows, and financial literacy statistics.

Visual representation of data is an indispensable tool in research reporting. By using appropriate visualization techniques, researchers can effectively communicate their findings, engage their audience, and provide actionable insights. In the Indian context, where diverse stakeholders require accessible and impactful data, visualization ensures inclusivity and clarity.

References

Borgatti, S. P., Everett, M. G., & Johnson, J. C. (2018). *Analyzing social networks*. SAGE Publications.

Goodfellow, I., Bengio, Y., & Courville, A. (2016). *Deep learning*. MIT Press.

Kozinets, R. V. (2015). *Netnography: Redefined*. SAGE Publications.

Pang, B., & Lee, L. (2008). Opinion mining and sentiment analysis. *Foundations and Trends in Information Retrieval*, 2(1–2), 1–135.

Tashakkori, A., & Teddlie, C. (2010). *SAGE handbook of mixed methods in social & behavioral research*. SAGE Publications.

Yin, R. K. (2018). *Case study research and applications: Design and methods*. SAGE Publications.

The Future of Research in a Globalized and Technology-Driven World

Sonal, a public policy researcher, was intrigued by how global trends in education were shaping policy decisions in India. Her initial study focused on traditional methods like surveys and focus groups. However, she soon realized that global challenges—like access to online education during the COVID-19 pandemic—required innovative approaches. She began leveraging global datasets, artificial intelligence, and cross-cultural collaborations. This allowed her to not only address local issues but also contribute to broader global conversations.

Sonal's experience highlights the dynamic nature of research in today's interconnected world, where technology, globalization, and cross-disciplinary collaboration are reshaping the way we approach problems. This chapter explores key trends, opportunities, and challenges in the future of research.

Key Trends in Modern Research

1. Global Collaboration

Description

The rise of digital communication tools and global networks has made it easier for researchers from different countries to collaborate. Shared knowledge, datasets, and methodologies enable studies that transcend national boundaries.

Examples

- **Global Health**: Collaborative research on vaccines for COVID-19, involving scientists from around the world.
- **Climate Change**: Joint studies by institutions across continents on global warming impacts.

Tools for Collaboration

- **Platforms**: ResearchGate, Mendeley, and Slack.
- **Conferences**: Virtual academic conferences and webinars connecting researchers globally.

Benefits

- Diverse perspectives improve problem-solving.
- Access to international funding and datasets.

2. Big Data and Analytics

Description

The ability to process and analyze large datasets is transforming research across disciplines. Big data allows researchers to uncover patterns and trends that were previously inaccessible.

Applications

- **Social Sciences**: Analyzing social media trends to understand public opinion.
- **Management**: Using sales data to predict market trends.

Tools

- Hadoop, Apache Spark, and Google BigQuery.

Challenges

- Ethical concerns over data privacy and misuse.
- Skill gaps in data science among researchers.

3. Artificial Intelligence (AI) in Research

Description

AI is enhancing research methodologies by automating repetitive tasks, analyzing data, and generating predictions. It is especially valuable in disciplines requiring complex analysis, such as healthcare and finance.

Applications

- **Healthcare**: AI algorithms for disease diagnosis using patient data.
- **Education**: Personalizing e-learning content based on student performance.

Examples

- Predictive modeling for stock market trends using machine learning.
- Chatbots for automated survey administration in remote areas.

4. Interdisciplinary and Transdisciplinary Research
Description

Complex global issues require solutions that draw from multiple disciplines. Interdisciplinary research integrates concepts from various fields, while transdisciplinary research includes non-academic stakeholders like policymakers and communities.

Examples

- **Sustainable Development**: Combining environmental science, economics, and social policy.
- **Smart Cities**: Integrating urban planning, technology, and sociology.

Benefits

- Holistic approaches to problem-solving.
- Increased relevance to real-world challenges.

Challenges

- Coordination among diverse teams.
- Balancing theoretical rigor with practical application.

5. Citizen Science

Description

Citizen science involves the public in research projects, often through data collection, analysis, or problem-solving.

Examples

- **Astronomy**: Amateur astronomers contributing to star mapping projects.
- **Environmental Studies**: Local communities monitoring air and water quality.

Tools

- Platforms like Zooniverse and iNaturalist.

Benefits

- Expands the scale and scope of research.
- Encourages public engagement with science.

Opportunities in a Technology-Driven World

1. Access to Global Datasets

- Platforms like the United Nations Data Hub and World Bank Databases provide extensive datasets.
- Researchers can analyze global trends without conducting primary data collection.

2. Automation of Repetitive Tasks

- AI tools like NVivo automate qualitative data coding, while SPSS accelerates statistical analysis.
- Saves time for complex tasks like hypothesis testing or model building.

3. Open Access Movement

- Open access journals and repositories make research findings widely available.
- Examples: PLOS ONE, arXiv, and PubMed Central.

Challenges in Future Research

1. Ethical Concerns in Technology-Driven Research

Description

The rise of big data and AI has led to concerns about privacy, consent, and algorithmic bias.
Example

- Misuse of personal data collected from social media platforms.

Solutions

- Stronger regulations like GDPR.
- Developing ethical guidelines for AI in research.

2. Digital Divide

Description

Unequal access to technology creates disparities in who can participate in or benefit from research.
Example

- Researchers in developing countries may lack access to advanced tools like high-performance computing.

Solutions

- Initiatives like the Global Research Council, which promote equitable access to resources.

3. Managing Interdisciplinary Complexity

Description

Combining methodologies and perspectives from multiple disciplines can lead to conflicts and misalignment.
Example

- Economists and environmentalists may have differing priorities when studying sustainable development.

Solutions

- Clear communication and shared goals among team members.

Emerging Technologies Shaping Research

1. Blockchain for Research Integrity

- Blockchain can secure research data, ensuring its authenticity and transparency.
- Example: Storing clinical trial data on blockchain to prevent manipulation.

2. Virtual and Augmented Reality (VR/AR)

- VR/AR technologies enable immersive experiments in fields like education and psychology.
- Example: Simulating disaster scenarios to study human behavior.

Real-World Applications

Case Study: Climate Change Research

Objective: To study the impact of rising sea levels on coastal communities.
  Approach:

1. **Big Data**: Using satellite imagery to map vulnerable areas.
2. **Interdisciplinary Research**: Combining climate science, economics, and sociology.
3. **Citizen Science**: Engaging local communities to monitor coastal erosion.

Outcome: Comprehensive recommendations for sustainable coastal management.

The future of research is marked by innovation, collaboration, and inclusivity. By embracing advanced methodologies and addressing emerging challenges, researchers can generate impactful solutions to global problems. In this interconnected and technology-driven era, the possibilities for transformative research are boundless.

References

Bryman, A. (2015). *Social research methods* (5th ed.). Oxford University Press.

Floridi, L. (2019). *Ethics of artificial intelligence: A critical review*. Springer.

Goodfellow, I., Bengio, Y., & Courville, A. (2016). *Deep learning*. MIT Press.

Kozinets, R. V. (2015). *Netnography: Redefined*. SAGE Publications.

Repko, A. F., & Szostak, R. (2020). *Interdisciplinary research: Process and theory*. SAGE Publications.

Tashakkori, A., & Teddlie, C. (2010). *SAGE handbook of mixed methods in social & behavioral research*. SAGE Publications.

Yin, R. K. (2018). *Case study research and applications: Design and methods*. SAGE Publications.

CHAPTER XIII

Writing a Research Proposal

A research proposal is the blueprint of your study, serving as both a roadmap for your work and a tool to secure approval or funding. It demonstrates the relevance, feasibility, and rigor of your research. Crafting a strong proposal is crucial for convincing supervisors, institutions, or sponsors of your study's value.

Importance of a Research Proposal

A well-written research proposal lays the groundwork for your study by defining objectives, outlining methodologies, and addressing potential challenges. It enables the researcher to:

1. Clarify the scope and focus of the research.
2. Highlight the significance of the study in addressing knowledge gaps.
3. Plan resources effectively, including time, funding, and personnel.
4. Ensure alignment with ethical standards and institutional requirements.
5. Secure approval from academic or funding bodies.

Writing a proposal also serves as an intellectual exercise, allowing researchers to refine their research questions and methodologies before data collection begins (Creswell & Creswell, 2018).

Components of a Research Proposal

1. Title

The title should be concise, specific, and indicative of the study's focus. It should capture the essence of the research while being engaging. For example, instead of a vague title like "Employee Behavior," a clearer one could be: "The Impact of Transformational Leadership on Employee Motivation in the Indian IT Sector."

2. Introduction

The introduction sets the stage by providing background information and defining the research problem. Start with an engaging hook, such as a compelling statistic or a real-world example, to establish the relevance of the study. This section should also explain the rationale for the research and its expected contributions to the field.

Example: "In the dynamic landscape of the Indian IT sector, employee motivation remains a critical factor influencing organizational success. Despite extensive research on leadership styles, little is known about how transformational leadership specifically affects motivation in this context. This study aims to address this gap."

3. Literature Review

The literature review contextualizes your study within existing research. It identifies gaps, debates, and unresolved questions, thereby justifying the need for your study. Organize this section thematically, grouping similar studies together. For instance, you might first discuss studies on transformational leadership, followed by those on employee motivation, and conclude with gaps in Indian contexts.

Cite recent and relevant sources to establish credibility. For example, include foundational works like Bass's (1990) theory of transformational leadership and more recent studies that examine its cultural applicability (Breevaart & Bakker, 2018).

4. Research Objectives

Clearly state what the study aims to achieve. Objectives should be specific, measurable, achievable, relevant, and time-bound (SMART). For example:

- To examine the relationship between transformational leadership and employee motivation.
- To analyze the mediating role of job satisfaction in this relationship.

5. Research Questions and Hypotheses

State your research questions and hypotheses based on your objectives. Research questions guide the study, while hypotheses provide testable statements.

Example:

- **Research Question**: How does transformational leadership influence employee motivation in the Indian IT sector?
- **Hypothesis**: Transformational leadership positively affects employee motivation, mediated by job satisfaction.

6. Methodology

The methodology section outlines how the research will be conducted. This includes the research design, data collection methods, sampling techniques, and tools for analysis.

1. **Research Design**: Specify whether the study is exploratory, descriptive, or causal. For instance, a causal design would be appropriate for testing the hypothesis about leadership and motivation.
2. **Population and Sampling**: Describe the target population and sampling technique. For example, you might use stratified random sampling to ensure representation across junior, mid-level, and senior employees.
3. **Data Collection**: Detail the instruments and techniques. For instance, surveys with a 5-point Likert scale could measure motivation levels, while interviews provide qualitative insights.
4. **Data Analysis**: Explain the tools and techniques for analysis. Statistical methods such as regression analysis might be used to test relationships, while thematic analysis could interpret qualitative data.

7. Ethical Considerations

Discuss how the study will ensure informed consent, confidentiality, and avoidance of harm. This section should address how ethical challenges will be mitigated, such as anonymizing data or providing participants with the right to withdraw (Bryman, 2015).

8. Timeline

Include a timeline that divides the research process into phases, such as literature review, data collection, analysis, and reporting. A Gantt chart can visually represent this timeline, aiding clarity.

9. Budget

If the proposal is for funding, include a detailed budget. Break down costs into categories such as data collection, software, travel, and personnel. For example:

- Data collection (survey distribution): ₹30,000
- Statistical software (SPSS license): ₹10,000
- Travel to case study locations: ₹20,000

10. Expected Outcomes

Outline the anticipated findings and their implications for academia, practice, or policy. For instance, "This study is expected to demonstrate the critical role of transformational leadership in enhancing motivation, providing actionable insights for HR managers in the IT sector."

11. References

Include all sources cited in the proposal, formatted according to the required citation style, such as APA.

Types of Research Reports

Research reports vary based on their purpose, audience, and structure. Understanding these types helps researchers tailor their presentation to meet the needs of stakeholders effectively.

1. Technical Reports

Technical reports focus on detailed methodologies, data analysis, and findings. They are primarily intended for academic or professional audiences who seek in-depth insights.

Key Features:

- Comprehensive and data-driven.
- Includes extensive use of charts, tables, and appendices.
- Written in a formal and precise tone.

Example in India:

A technical report by the Reserve Bank of India (RBI) analyzing inflation trends in India over the past decade.

2. Management Reports

Management reports are designed to present actionable insights for decision makers. They summarize findings with a focus on implications and recommendations.

Key Features:

- Concise and focused on practical outcomes.
- Highlights key findings and actionable steps.
- Includes executive summaries and visual aids.

Example in India:

A report for Infosys management analyzing employee retention strategies based on internal surveys.

3. Popular Reports

Popular reports are created for a general audience. They present findings in an accessible manner, often with simplified language and engaging visuals.

Key Features:

- Focuses on storytelling and narrative style.
- Limited use of technical jargon.
- Includes visuals like infographics and simple charts.

Example in India:

A report on the benefits of renewable energy adoption published by the Ministry of New and Renewable Energy (MNRE) for public awareness.

4. Policy Reports

Policy reports are intended for government bodies or policymakers. They include recommendations based on research findings to guide public policies.

Key Features:

- Emphasizes relevance to policy goals.
- Contains clear recommendations and supporting evidence.
- Often includes cost-benefit analysis.

Example in India:

A NITI Aayog report recommending strategies for improving digital literacy in rural India.

5. Research Articles

Research articles are condensed reports of studies published in academic journals. They target scholarly audiences and contribute to academic discourse.

Key Features:

- Follows a strict structure (Abstract, Introduction, Methods, Results, Discussion, Conclusion).
- Peer-reviewed to ensure quality and credibility.

Example:

A research article in the Indian Journal of Marketing analyzing the impact of influencer marketing on Gen Z consumers.

6. Feasibility Reports

Feasibility reports evaluate the viability of proposed projects or initiatives. They focus on practicality, risks, and expected outcomes.

Key Features:

- Includes financial and operational analysis.
- Highlights potential risks and solutions.
- Concludes with a recommendation.

Example in India:

A feasibility report on introducing electric buses in Bengaluru by the Karnataka State Road Transport Corporation (KSRTC).

7. Evaluation Reports

Evaluation reports assess the effectiveness of implemented projects or policies, often comparing outcomes against predefined goals.

Key Features:

- Focuses on measuring success and impact.
- Includes qualitative and quantitative assessments.
- Offers lessons learned for future improvements.

Example:

An evaluation report by the Indian government on the effectiveness of the Swachh Bharat Mission.

Choosing the Right Report Type

1. **Understand the Audience:**

   Match the report type to the audience's expectations. For example, technical reports are better suited for experts, while popular reports cater to the general public.

2. **Define the Purpose:**

   Align the structure and content of the report with its objectives, whether academic, managerial, or policy-oriented.

3. **Use Appropriate Language:**

   Adapt the tone and complexity of language to ensure clarity and engagement for the target audience.

Importance of Tailored Reports

1. **Effective Communication:**
   Presenting findings in the right format ensures the message resonates with the audience.
2. **Enhanced Decision-Making:**
   Management and policy reports provide actionable insights, leading to informed decisions.
3. **Broader Reach:**
   Popular and public-facing reports help disseminate knowledge to non-technical audiences.

Real-World Applications in India

1. **Academic Research:**
   Universities like IITs publish technical reports and journal articles on innovations and scientific breakthroughs.
2. **Corporate Strategy:**
   Companies like Tata Group use management reports to inform business strategy and performance evaluations.
3. **Public Awareness Campaigns:**
   Organizations like TERI (The Energy and Resources Institute) release popular reports on climate change to educate the public.

Understanding the types of research reports enables researchers to tailor their findings for diverse audiences, ensuring effective communication and practical application. Whether it's influencing policy, guiding business decisions, or contributing to academic knowledge, selecting the appropriate report format is a critical step in the research process.

Tips for Writing a Strong Proposal

1. **Know Your Audience**: Tailor the proposal to the expectations of the approving body, whether it's a university committee, funding agency, or corporate sponsor.
2. **Be Concise and Specific**: Avoid vague language and focus on clear, measurable objectives.
3. **Use Visuals**: Incorporate tables, charts, or graphs to enhance clarity. For example, use a chart to compare different sampling methods.
4. **Address Feasibility**: Acknowledge potential challenges and how you plan to overcome them, such as limited access to participants or funding constraints.
5. **Proofread Thoroughly**: Ensure the proposal is free of grammatical errors and inconsistencies, as these can undermine credibility.

Example Proposal Overview

Title: "Exploring the Impact of Social Media Marketing on Consumer Behavior: A Study of Indian Millennials"
Introduction: This study examines how social media marketing influences purchasing decisions among Indian millennials, a demographic characterized by high digital engagement.
Objectives:

- To analyze the effectiveness of influencer campaigns.
- To assess the role of platform-specific features (e.g., Instagram reels, Facebook ads).

Methodology:

- Mixed-methods approach, combining quantitative surveys with qualitative netnographic analysis of social media discussions.
- Sample size: 500 respondents aged 18–35.

Expected Outcomes:

- Insights into consumer preferences for different types of social media content.
- Recommendations for brands targeting millennials.

A research proposal is more than a formal document—it's a strategic plan that defines the purpose, scope, and feasibility of your study. By addressing all essential components and tailoring your proposal to its intended audience, you can secure the approval and resources necessary for successful research.

References

Bass, B. M. (1990). *Bass & Stogdill's handbook of leadership: Theory, research, and managerial applications*. Free Press.
Breevaart, K., & Bakker, A. B. (2018). Daily job demands and employee engagement: The role of daily transformational leadership behavior. *Journal of Occupational Health Psychology, 23*(3), 338–349.
Bryman, A. (2015). *Social research methods* (5th ed.). Oxford University Press.
Creswell, J. W., & Creswell, J. D. (2018). *Research design: Qualitative, quantitative, and mixed methods approaches* (5th ed.). Sage Publications.

CHAPTER XIV

Writing and Publishing Research Papers

Writing and publishing research papers is a vital step in disseminating knowledge, contributing to academic discourse, and building a researcher's professional profile. A well-written paper effectively communicates your research findings, while publishing ensures that your work reaches relevant audiences, including scholars, practitioners, and policymakers.

Importance of Research Paper Writing and Publishing

1. **Disseminates Knowledge**: Papers share new findings, theories, or methodologies, advancing the field of study (Creswell & Creswell, 2018).
2. **Establishes Credibility**: Publishing in reputable journals demonstrates expertise and enhances a researcher's academic standing.
3. **Promotes Collaboration**: Published work sparks discussions and collaborations among researchers globally.
4. **Impacts Policy and Practice**: Research papers influence decision-making in industries and governance.
5. **Fulfills Academic Requirements**: Many graduate programs and funding agencies require publishing as part of their criteria.

Structure of a Research Paper

A standard research paper follows a structured format, typically outlined below:

1. Title

The title is the first impression of your research. It should be concise, specific, and engaging, reflecting the paper's focus. For example: "Digital Payment Adoption in Rural India: Determinants and Challenges."

2. Abstract

The abstract summarizes the research in 200–300 words, including the problem, objectives, methods, key findings, and implications.

Example:

"This study examines the adoption of digital payment systems in rural India, focusing on socio-economic determinants and infrastructural challenges. Using surveys of 500 households and interviews with stakeholders, the study reveals that literacy, smartphone penetration, and trust significantly influence adoption. Recommendations include targeted awareness campaigns and investment in digital infrastructure."

3. Introduction

The introduction provides background information, the research problem, and the paper's objectives. A strong introduction hooks the reader and explains why the study is relevant.

4. Literature Review

This section contextualizes the study by discussing existing research. Highlight gaps and explain how your paper addresses them. For instance, if previous studies focus on urban areas, your work on rural India fills an important void.

5. Methodology

Describe the research design, sampling methods, data collection tools, and analytical techniques in detail. Transparency in this section allows other researchers to replicate your study.

6. Results

Present your findings using text, tables, and visuals. For quantitative studies, include statistical analyses like regression coefficients or correlation matrices. In qualitative studies, summarize themes and patterns.

7. Discussion

Interpret your findings in relation to your research objectives and existing literature. Explain anomalies, unexpected results, or limitations and their implications.

8. Conclusion

Summarize key findings, their significance, and practical applications. Include recommendations and suggestions for future research.

9. References

Cite all sources in a consistent format (e.g., APA, MLA). Include recent and authoritative references to establish credibility.

Writing Tips for Research Papers

1. **Plan and Outline**

   - Develop a clear outline before writing to ensure logical flow and comprehensive coverage.

2. **Use Clear Language**

   - Avoid jargon and write in a straightforward, concise manner. Aim for accessibility without sacrificing precision.

3. **Be Objective**

   - Present findings neutrally, supported by data, without exaggeration or bias.

4. **Edit and Revise**

   - Review your draft multiple times for coherence, grammar, and consistency. Consider peer feedback for improvement.

5. **Focus on Visuals**

   - Use graphs, charts, and tables effectively to complement your findings. Ensure visuals are labeled and easy to interpret.

Choosing the Right Journal

Publishing success largely depends on selecting a suitable journal. Factors to consider include:

1. **Scope and Audience**

   - Match your paper's subject matter with the journal's focus. For instance, a paper on consumer behavior might align with the *Journal of Consumer Research*.

2. **Impact Factor**

   ◦ High-impact journals like *Nature* or *Science* enhance visibility but have rigorous standards.

3. **Open Access vs. Subscription-Based**

   ◦ Open access journals make your work freely available, increasing reach. Examples include *PLOS ONE*.

4. **Publication Speed**

   ◦ For time-sensitive studies, consider journals with shorter review cycles.

The Peer Review Process

Peer review ensures the quality and validity of published research. Understanding the process can help researchers navigate it effectively:

1. **Submission**: Submit the manuscript along with supplementary materials, such as datasets or appendices, if required.
2. **Initial Screening**: The journal editor assesses the paper's fit for the journal's scope and quality standards.
3. **Peer Review**: Experts in the field evaluate the manuscript for originality, rigor, and significance.
4. **Revisions**: Address reviewers' comments and resubmit the revised manuscript.
5. **Decision**: The editor decides to accept, reject, or request further revisions.

Rejection is common, especially in competitive journals. Constructive feedback should guide improvements for resubmission elsewhere.

Ethical Considerations in Publishing

1. **Avoid Plagiarism**

   ◦ Cite all sources accurately and ensure originality. Tools like Turnitin or Grammarly can help identify unintentional plagiarism.

2. **Disclose Conflicts of Interest**

   ◦ Declare any affiliations or funding sources that might bias the research.

3. **Authorship Criteria**

   ◦ Only include individuals who made significant contributions to the study.

4. **Avoid Duplicate Submission**

   ◦ Do not submit the same manuscript to multiple journals simultaneously.

5. **Adhere to Data Integrity**

   ◦ Report data truthfully, without manipulation or fabrication.

Real-World Example

Research Topic: "Understanding the Gender Gap in Entrepreneurship in South Asia"

1. **Abstract**: Summarizes the gender gap in entrepreneurship, identifying barriers like societal norms and limited access to capital.
2. **Methodology**: Combines surveys with 500 women entrepreneurs and interviews with policymakers.
3. **Findings**: Women entrepreneurs face higher barriers to credit access compared to men. Education and mentorship significantly mitigate these challenges.
4. **Publication**: Published in the *International Journal of Entrepreneurship and Small Business.*

Writing and publishing research papers is an iterative process that demands clarity, precision, and adherence to ethical standards. By following structured guidelines and understanding journal requirements, researchers can effectively share their findings, contribute to their fields, and influence broader discussions in academia and practice.

Effective Presentation Techniques for Research Findings

Presenting research findings effectively ensures that insights are understood, appreciated, and actionable. A well-crafted presentation not only highlights key outcomes but also persuades stakeholders to take informed decisions.

Key Components of a Research Presentation

1. **Define the Audience:**
   Understanding the audience's needs and knowledge level helps tailor the content.

   ◦ **Example in India:** A corporate team might prioritize financial impacts, while policymakers focus on societal benefits.

2. **Set Clear Objectives:**
   The presentation should align with the purpose of the research, whether it's to inform, persuade, or make recommendations.

   ◦ **Example:** A presentation for the Ministry of Health may emphasize actionable recommendations for improving vaccination rates.

3. **Structure the Presentation:**

   ◦ **Introduction:** Context, research objectives, and scope.
   ◦ **Methods:** Key details on data collection and analysis techniques.
   ◦ **Results:** Use visuals to highlight trends, relationships, or key findings.
   ◦ **Conclusions and Recommendations:** Summarize insights and suggest actionable steps.

Visual Tools for Presentations

1. **Slideshows (e.g., PowerPoint, Google Slides):**

   - Use concise text and visuals.
   - Avoid clutter by limiting slides to one main idea each.
   - Include graphs, images, and bullet points.

   Example: A slide presenting growth trends in India's e-commerce sector using a line graph.

1. **Charts and Graphs:**

   - Use bar charts, line graphs, pie charts, and histograms to display quantitative data.
   - Ensure clear labeling and appropriate color schemes.
   - Highlight key trends or outliers with annotations.

   Example: A pie chart showing market share distribution among telecom providers (Jio, Airtel, Vodafone).

3. **Infographics:**

   - Combine visuals and text for impactful storytelling.
   - Ideal for presenting summaries or overviews.

   Example: An infographic summarizing the benefits of renewable energy adoption in India.

4. **Interactive Dashboards (e.g., Tableau, Power BI):**

   - Use dynamic visuals for real-time exploration of data.
   - Great for business or technical presentations.

   Example: A Tableau dashboard showing real-time data on COVID-19 cases across Indian states.

5. **Posters and Reports:**

   - Effective for academic and public events.
   - Include concise sections, visuals, and contact information.

   Delivery Techniques

1. **Engage the Audience:**

   - Use storytelling to connect with the audience emotionally.
   - Involve the audience through questions or discussions.

   Example: A presenter might share a success story about digital payments improving lives in rural India.

2. **Practice Clarity and Simplicity:**

   - Avoid technical jargon unless necessary.
   - Use simple language to explain complex concepts.

3. **Use Timing Effectively:**

   - Limit the presentation to the allotted time.
   - Allocate time for Q&A to address audience concerns.

4. **Body Language and Voice:**

   - Maintain eye contact, use gestures, and modulate voice to emphasize key points.

5. **Rehearse and Adapt:**

   - Practice multiple times to refine the flow.
   - Be ready to adapt based on audience reactions or feedback.

Common Pitfalls to Avoid

1. **Overloading Slides:**
   Too much text or data distracts from the main message.
2. **Ignoring Audience Needs:**
   A presentation focused only on data might lose non-technical stakeholders.
3. **Neglecting Visual Quality:**
   Poor design, inconsistent formatting, or unreadable text can undermine credibility.

Real-World Applications in India

1. **Corporate Strategy Meetings:**
   A presentation for Tata Group might include dashboards and scenario-based visuals to support strategic decisions.
2. **Government Policy Briefings:**
   A researcher presenting findings on urban traffic congestion to NITI Aayog could use heat maps and projections.
3. **Public Awareness Campaigns:**
   NGOs like Pratham use infographics and storytelling to highlight the impact of their educational initiatives.

An effective presentation is more than just delivering data—it's about engaging the audience, highlighting key insights, and driving action. By leveraging visual tools, clear structuring, and engaging delivery techniques, researchers can ensure their findings leave a lasting impact. Tailored approaches are particularly crucial in India's diverse settings, where stakeholders range from policymakers and corporate leaders to the general public.

References

Creswell, J. W., & Creswell, J. D. (2018). *Research design: Qualitative, quantitative, and mixed methods approaches* (5th ed.). Sage Publications.
Bryman, A. (2015). *Social research methods* (5th ed.). Oxford University Press.
Zikmund, W. G., Babin, B. J., Carr, J. C., & Griffin, M. (2013). *Business research methods*. Cengage Learning.
PLOS ONE. (n.d.). Retrieved from https://journals.plos.org/plosone/
Nature. (n.d.). Retrieved from https://www.nature.com/
Turnitin. (n.d.). Retrieved from https://www.turnitin.com/

CHAPTER XV

Research Dissemination and Impact

After completing and publishing a research study, the next step is ensuring that its findings reach the right audience and create a meaningful impact. Dissemination involves sharing research outcomes with stakeholders, including academics, practitioners, policymakers, and the public, while ensuring the study's practical or theoretical contributions are fully realized.

Importance of Research Dissemination

1. **Maximizes Reach**: Ensures research findings are accessible to relevant audiences, increasing their influence on decisions or further studies (Creswell & Plano Clark, 2017).
2. **Encourages Application**: Facilitates the translation of findings into policies, practices, or innovations.
3. **Inspires Collaboration**: Stimulates interdisciplinary or cross-sectoral collaborations for future research.
4. **Enhances Reputation**: Establishes the researcher as an expert in their field.
5. **Supports Funding Goals**: Demonstrates the impact of funded research, increasing chances of future grants.

Methods of Dissemination

1. Academic Platforms

Academic dissemination ensures findings contribute to the existing body of knowledge.

- **Journals**: Publish in peer-reviewed journals with high relevance and impact.
- **Conferences**: Present findings at international, national, or regional conferences. These venues provide networking opportunities and feedback.
- **Books and Chapters**: Expand on research by authoring books or contributing chapters to edited volumes.

2. Digital Media

Digital tools enable broader dissemination and engagement with non-academic audiences.

- **Open Access Repositories**: Upload papers to platforms like ResearchGate or institutional repositories to ensure free access.
- **Social Media**: Share summaries or infographics on platforms like Twitter, LinkedIn, or Instagram to reach diverse groups.
- **Webinars and Podcasts**: Host or participate in virtual discussions to explain findings in an accessible format.

3. Policy Briefs

Tailored for policymakers, policy briefs summarize research findings, implications, and recommendations concisely.

Example: A policy brief on education access in rural areas could highlight key barriers and propose actionable solutions like digital learning initiatives.

4. Community Engagement

Collaborate with community groups, NGOs, or local leaders to share findings directly with affected populations. This can involve workshops, public presentations, or co-creating solutions.

5. Media Outreach

Engage traditional media outlets to amplify research findings. Write op-eds, appear on news shows, or partner with journalists to cover the study's impact.

Evaluating Research Impact

Assessing impact helps researchers understand how their work influences academic, social, or economic spheres.

1. Academic Impact

- **Metrics**: Citation counts, journal impact factors, and h-index scores reflect scholarly influence.
- **Collaborations**: Invitations for joint research projects or keynote speeches indicate recognition.

2. Social Impact

- **Policy Changes**: Research that informs or modifies policy demonstrates societal relevance.
- **Behavioral Shifts**: Studies on public health, education, or environment that lead to measurable changes.

3. Economic Impact

- **Innovation**: Research that drives new technologies, patents, or business models.
- **Cost Savings**: Studies that optimize processes or improve resource allocation.

4. Public Engagement

- **Media Coverage**: Frequency and tone of media reports on the research.
- **Community Feedback**: Reactions from stakeholders or participants in workshops.

Challenges in Dissemination

1. **Audience Mismatch**

   - Research may not be tailored to the needs or understanding of specific audiences.
   - **Solution**: Adjust communication style and format for different groups.

2. **Limited Access**

   - Paywalls or subscription-based journals restrict public access to findings.
   - **Solution**: Use open-access publishing or upload preprints to repositories.

3. **Time and Resources**

   - Dissemination can be time-intensive, especially for outreach activities.
   - **Solution**: Include dissemination plans and budgets in research proposals.

4. **Cultural Barriers**

- ○ Cross-cultural studies may face challenges in translating findings into actionable insights for diverse groups.
- ○ **Solution**: Engage local stakeholders early in the research process.

Real-World Example

Case Study: Disseminating Research on Clean Energy Adoption

1. **Publication**: Published in the *Journal of Environmental Economics*.
2. **Conference Presentation**: Presented at a global clean energy summit, sparking collaborations with renewable energy firms.
3. **Policy Brief**: Shared findings with government ministries, leading to subsidies for solar panel adoption in rural areas.
4. **Community Workshop**: Conducted sessions in rural districts to demonstrate cost-saving benefits of solar energy.
5. **Digital Outreach**: Shared infographics on social media, engaging thousands of followers and receiving media coverage.

Research dissemination is the bridge between knowledge creation and its application in the real world. By leveraging academic platforms, digital media, community engagement, and policy advocacy, researchers can maximize the impact of their work. In the next chapter, we will reflect on the overall journey of conducting social science research and provide a roadmap for aspiring researchers.

Emerging Trends in Research Methodology

The field of research methodology is evolving rapidly, driven by technological advancements and changing research needs. These emerging trends are reshaping how data is collected, analyzed, and interpreted, making research more efficient and impactful.

1. Big Data Analytics

Big data analytics involves processing and analyzing large datasets to uncover patterns, trends, and insights.

Applications:

- Predicting consumer behavior based on online activities.
- Monitoring real-time trends in public health or social media.

Example in India:

E-commerce platforms like Amazon India use big data to personalize customer experiences and optimize supply chains.

2. Artificial Intelligence (AI) and Machine Learning (ML)

AI and ML are revolutionizing research by automating data analysis, identifying patterns, and generating predictive models.

Applications:

- Sentiment analysis in social media research.
- Predictive modeling in financial markets.

Example in India:

Banks like HDFC and ICICI use AI-driven models to assess credit risks and detect fraudulent transactions.

3. Mixed-Methods Research

Mixed-methods research combines qualitative and quantitative approaches, providing a comprehensive understanding of complex problems.

Applications:

- Evaluating the effectiveness of education policies.
- Understanding customer satisfaction through surveys and interviews.

Example in India:

A study on smart city initiatives might combine household surveys (quantitative) with focus group discussions (qualitative).

4. Digital Ethnography

Digital ethnography studies online communities, behaviors, and interactions. It is particularly relevant for understanding virtual environments.

Applications:

- Analyzing social media behavior.
- Studying e-commerce user experiences.

Example in India:

Researchers studying political trends might analyze Twitter and Facebook discussions during elections.

5. Blockchain for Research Integrity

Blockchain technology ensures data security, transparency, and integrity in research processes.

Applications:

- Maintaining secure records of clinical trial data.
- Verifying the authenticity of published findings.

Example in India:

Healthcare research institutions might use blockchain to secure patient data during large-scale studies.

6. Remote Data Collection Tools

With increasing digitization, online surveys, mobile apps, and telephonic interviews have become popular for data collection.

Applications:

- Conducting nationwide surveys efficiently.
- Reaching rural and remote populations.

Example in India:

The Indian government uses mobile apps like mAadhaar for population studies and welfare monitoring.

7. Data Visualization and Dashboards

Advanced visualization tools like Tableau and Power BI make it easier to present complex data in interactive and engaging formats.

Applications:

- Creating dashboards for policymaker briefings.
- Sharing real-time insights with stakeholders.

Example in India:

A dashboard tracking renewable energy adoption in India across states, used by the Ministry of Power.

8. Sustainability and Green Research

Sustainability-focused research emphasizes minimizing the environmental impact of research activities, including digital footprints and resource usage.

Applications:

- Using eco-friendly practices in field studies.
- Analyzing the environmental impacts of policies.

Example in India:

Research on India's plastic waste management policies might emphasize green methodologies for data collection and analysis.

9. Gamification in Surveys

Gamification makes surveys engaging by incorporating game-like elements, increasing response rates and data quality.

Applications:

- Gathering data on consumer preferences.
- Studying youth behaviors through interactive methods.

Example in India:

An edtech company like BYJU'S might gamify surveys to collect feedback from students.

10. Internet of Things (IoT) in Research

IoT devices enable automated data collection from connected systems, providing real-time and accurate data.

Applications:

- Monitoring smart agriculture systems.
- Studying energy usage patterns in smart cities.

Example in India:

IoT-enabled devices might be used to study water usage efficiency in drought-prone areas of Rajasthan.

Benefits of Emerging Trends

1. **Efficiency:**

   Technologies like AI and IoT streamline data collection and analysis, reducing time and effort.

2. **Accuracy:**

   Big data and advanced analytics improve the reliability of research findings.

3. **Scalability:**

   Digital tools enable large-scale studies, making it easier to analyze trends across diverse populations.

4. **Accessibility:**

   Remote tools and online platforms increase accessibility to previously hard-to-reach populations.

Challenges and Ethical Considerations

1. **Data Privacy:**

   Protecting sensitive information is crucial, especially in digital and IoT-driven research.

2. **Digital Divide:**
   Access to technology remains uneven, particularly in rural India.
3. **Bias in AI Models:**
   Algorithms can perpetuate biases if not designed carefully.

Emerging trends in research methodology are transforming the research landscape, enabling more robust, efficient, and inclusive studies. In the Indian context, leveraging these advancements can help address diverse challenges, from urban development to rural empowerment. By embracing these trends while addressing their ethical implications, researchers can stay at the forefront of innovation and impact.

References

Creswell, J. W., & Plano Clark, V. L. (2017). *Designing and conducting mixed methods research* (3rd ed.). Sage Publications.
Zikmund, W. G., Babin, B. J., Carr, J. C., & Griffin, M. (2013). *Business research methods.* Cengage Learning.

Epilogue: Embarking On Your Research Journey

As you close this book, remember that research is not merely a process of answering questions; it is a quest for understanding, a way to contribute to the world, and an opportunity to grow intellectually. The chapters you have explored—from identifying research problems to disseminating findings—are your roadmap for conducting meaningful research in the social sciences.

Key Takeaways

1. **The Power of Curiosity**

   - All research begins with curiosity. The desire to question the status quo and seek evidence-based answers is what drives impactful research.

2. **The Role of Systematic Thinking**

   - Whether choosing a methodology or analyzing data, the ability to think systematically and critically is your most valuable tool.

3. **Collaboration and Community**

   - Research thrives on collaboration. Engage with peers, mentors, and stakeholders to refine your ideas and amplify your impact.

4. **Ethics and Responsibility**

   - Adhering to ethical principles ensures that your research respects participants, upholds integrity, and serves the greater good.

5. **Embracing Innovation**

   - In a world driven by technology and globalization, adopting advanced methodologies and embracing interdisciplinary approaches will set you apart.

6. **Impact and Legacy**

   - Your work has the potential to shape policies, inspire practices, and contribute to academic knowledge. Always aim for research that leaves a lasting impact.

The Future of Research

The landscape of research is evolving rapidly. Advances in artificial intelligence, big data, and collaborative platforms are opening new avenues for inquiry. As you move forward, stay informed about emerging trends, and be prepared to adapt your approaches to address the complexities of a changing world.

Final Words of Encouragement

Research is both a challenge and a privilege. There will be obstacles—uncooperative datasets, unanswered questions, and even rejections. But every step, whether it feels like progress or setback, is part of your growth as a researcher.

As you embark on your research journey, remember that every question you explore, every insight you uncover, and every solution you propose has the power to make a difference. Whether you are a novice or an experienced researcher, your work contributes to the collective effort to understand and improve our world.

So, go forth with confidence, curiosity, and commitment. The world of research awaits your contributions.

Final Note

This book has included 15 chapters, covering every stage of the research process in social sciences, with an emphasis on practical applications, advanced techniques, and the Indian context. Each chapter has been designed to equip you with the knowledge and skills to not only conduct research but also communicate it effectively and make a meaningful impact.

Your journey as a researcher does not end here—it begins now.